The Creative Copycat
II

THE CREATIVE COPYCAT
II

MARIAN L. CANOLES

Illustrations
by
Betty Ferguson Willcox

1985
Libraries Unlimited, Inc.
Littleton, Colorado

LIBRARIES UNLIMITED, INC.
P.O. Box 263
Littleton, Colorado 80160-0263

Library of Congress Cataloging in Publication Data

Canoles, Marian L., 1927-
   The creative copycat II.

   Bibliography: p. 179
   Includes index.
   1. Bulletin boards--Handbooks, manuals, etc.
   2. Holidays--United States--Handbooks, manuals, etc.
   3. Displays in education--Handbooks, manuals, etc.
   I. Title. II. Title: Creative copycat two. III. Title:
Creative copycat 2.
   LB1043.58.C37   1985   371.3'356   84-29994
   ISBN 0-87287-436-2

Libraries Unlimited books are bound with Type II nonwoven material that meets
and exceeds National Association of State Textbook Administrators' Type II nonwoven material specifications Class A through E.

—TABLE OF CONTENTS—

FALL *(cont'd)*

WINTER *(cont'd)*

—LIST OF PHOTOGRAPHS—

WINTER *(cont'd)*

–INTRODUCTION–

The Creative Copycat, published in 1982 by Libraries Unlimited, was conceived and created to fill the ongoing need of librarians and teachers for unique bulletin board ideas for the library and classroom. In a country which supports over 100,000 school and public libraries, however, a collection of 200 display ideas is negligible for librarians and teachers who must deal with the many factors involved in creating a monthly display. The availability of materials, quality of dependable assistance, time and skills involved, and need for variety all impose limits on their choices. *Copycat II* is intended to supplement *The Creative Copycat* with an additional selection of approximately 150 specialized board ideas.

Copycat II is of narrower scope than its predecessor. It concentrates on American holidays—26 in all—and the four seasons, as well as weekly and monthly observances like Black History Month, Children's Book Week, and National Library Week. (See Appendix 3 for dates of each event.) However, many of the ideas can be used in other contexts; for example, Goin' Steady, a Valentine's Day board on page 118, can be adapted to other themes, such as health or guidance, merely by changing the pocketed books. Several New Year's Day boards can be used at the beginning of the school year as well as in January. Lesser holidays have been included, such as Arbor Day, Groundhog Day, and Grandparents' Day. It is hoped that teachers, as well as librarians, will find the book useful.

As in *The Creative Copycat*, all bulletin boards are composed of inexpensive, available materials, the most important of which is paper. Appendix 1 of this book contains suggestions for materials and techniques, and the Annotated Bibliography consists almost exclusively of books on the subject of paperwork, all selected to be a working supplement to the text.

The bulletin board ideas here range from primary through high school levels. The instructions for each display contain suggestions for background color, type of lettering, method of construction, and materials needed. When a display is best suited to a large window, this is mentioned in the instructions. Easy-to-make boards are noted in the Table of Contents.

The Copycat figure appears throughout the pages of this book, mostly as a whimsical addition. Sometimes, however, her comments are an integral part of the bulletin board in question. You may want to substitute a cut-out drawing (on construction paper or posterboard) of your school mascot making Copycat's comment. (A small stuffed animal could be used for this purpose, also.) The same drawing or animal could be used repeatedly and only the speech balloon changed. The figure can simply be tacked to a corner of the bulletin board. In cases where Copycat's comment is essential to the board's message, include your Copycat substitute and the accompanying comment.

With the cooperation of Mrs. Ann Forster, Librarian, Norview High School, Norfolk, Virginia, I had the opportunity to assemble many of these displays throughout the school year. For this I am most thankful; it is necessary and desirable that these ideas be tried in the field.

A selection of photographs is included on pp. 63-74 to demonstrate how some drawings were converted to bulletin boards and to give credence to the fact that the drawings can indeed be transformed into bulletin boards. These pictures are included through the kindness of Walter R. Williamson, a freelance photographer who worked with the yearbook staff at Norview High School until his untimely death on November 3, 1984.

The steady, vitalizing support of my collaborator and good friend, Betty Willcox, has made the birthing of *Copycat II* both painless and joyful.

SUMMER

Flag Day

Father's Day

Grandparents'Day

Independence Day

Labor Day

School Opening

—FAR FROM THE MADDING CROWD—

BACKGROUND: White cotton batting.

LETTERING: Large—black cut-outs; small—black plastic.

METHOD & MATERIALS: Cut the small penguins from white construction paper. Sketch heads, wings, etc., with black marker. Use black construction paper for these parts of the large penguins, and make their bodies of shiny white posterboard; this improves the appearance of the foreground.

−GO ECLECTIC−

BACKGROUND: White paper or fabric.

LETTERING: Script−green yarn; other−black plastic.

METHOD & MATERIALS: Apply yellow corrugated border over white background. Cut large numerals (representing Dewey Decimal numbers) from nine different pieces of fabric scraps, varying both pattern and texture. Feature books from every category. Have summer reading lists available to hand out to students.

See photo, page 63.

–JUS' READIN'–

BACKGROUND: Top two-thirds—light blue paper; middle—dark blue; lower—tan.

LETTERING: Dark blue cut-outs.

METHOD & MATERIALS: Add more blue color and white clouds to the sky area, with chalk. In the same manner, sketch surf over middle area. Connote sand by stippling random areas with purple or pink chalk. Attach a hook to the approximate hat position on the finished board. Pin a piece of yellow-and-white-striped awning canvas cut in the shape of a trapezoid (the top wider than the bottom) to beach area. First tack lower corners, with right side of canvas against board. Next, turn material upward, allowing canvas to hang slightly. Now pin upper corner to surf area, allowing hook to protrude. Apply the back brace, made of corrugated paper strips. Add brown yarn ponytail, tied with a bow. Hang a large straw hat on the hook, secured with pins to prevent falling.

—SUNNY DAYS AHEAD—

BACKGROUND: Gray paper.

LETTERING: Book titles—cut-outs of various colors; other—black plastic or black cut-outs.

METHOD & MATERIALS: Cut eight or nine free forms from an assortment of colored construction paper, and the sun and its rays from yellow posterboard. Have letters of book titles contrast with the various background colors. This display is most effective on a very large board or as a background for a window exhibit.

—A CLASSY COUNTRY—

BACKGROUND: Light blue paper.

LETTERING: Large—white-on-black cut-outs; medium—black cut-outs; small—black plastic.

METHOD & MATERIALS: Cut out tuxedo-clad gent from black construction paper. Background paper serves as shirt front. Make studs and tie plain or fancy: draw with black felt pen, or glue on rhinestone buttons and pin on a real tie or one made with black crepe paper. Make or purchase a pink carnation for lapel. Add purchased American flag. Pin to give the appearance of blowing in the wind. This board is also usable for Independence Day.

—I AM WHAT YOU MAKE ME—

BACKGROUND: White paper or freezer wrapping paper.

LETTERING: Black cut-outs.

METHOD & MATERIALS: Before proceeding, consult an encyclopedia for exact representations of these three versions of the flag. Construct 1777 flag over white paper: tack on seven red crepe paper stripes, leaving six white stripes; superimpose a rectangle of blue construction paper; add white cut-out stars. Construct the two remaining flags—1818, with 20 stars, and present-day design—each on a corrugated base. Glue the small flag to that of 1818. When dry, superimpose on 1777 flag at center of board, securing with pins. Add lettering, "I am what you make me," along bottom of display.

—STATE FLAGS—

BACKGROUND: Red paper or fabric.

LETTERING: Large—black cut-outs; small—black plastic.

METHOD & MATERIALS: Make paper flags, relative to the size of your board, of several states. Hang each from a brass dowel; trim the ends of the dowels with yarn pulls. You might consider offering a prize to the student who identifies the flags first.

—A CELEBRATION OF FATHERS—

BACKGROUND: None necessary.

LETTERING: Tan-on-black cut-outs.

METHOD & MATERIALS: Prepare this board well in advance of June. Ask male school personnel for photos of themselves with their children. Pictures of famous men and their families can be used also. The point is to feature men your viewers will recognize. Cut black photo-mounting corners from construction paper.

—DADDY NEEDS—

BACKGROUND: White paper.

LETTERING: Script—yellow yarn; other—black plastic or yellow cut-outs edged with black pen.

METHOD & MATERIALS: Frame board with yellow corrugated edging. Arms and legs, made with various colors of construction paper, with details added in black marker, descend from behind the yellow frame.

Include Copycat's comment.

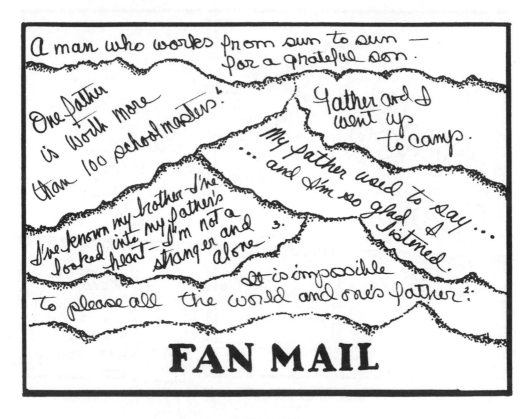

A man who works from sun to sun —
for a grateful son.

One father is worth more than 100 schoolmasters.[1]

Father and I went up to camp.

My father used to say... and I'm so glad I listened.

I've known my brother — I've looked into my father's heart — I'm not a stranger and alone.[3]

It is impossible to please all the world and one's father.[2]

FAN MAIL

—FAN MAIL—

BACKGROUND:	None.
LETTERING:	Script—colored felt pens; other—black cut-outs over white paper.
METHOD & MATERIALS:	Cover board, except for title area, with torn sheets of various colors of pastel paper. Vary handwriting in each section. This Father's Day board (perhaps more aptly called FAN MALE) displays short notes by students on the subject What My Father Means to Me, or famous quotations about fathers. It can be used at graduation time, also, with testimonials in praise of the school, written by graduating seniors.

[1] George Herbert, *Jacula Prudentum.*

[2] La Fontaine, *Fables.*

[3] Thomas Wolfe, *Look Homeward Angel* (paraphrase).

—FATHER KNOWS BEST—

BACKGROUND: Navy blue paper.

LETTERING: Large—kelly green cut-outs; small—white plastic or white yarn script.

METHOD & MATERIALS: On a long sheet of white posterboard, neatly list titles, characters, and authors related in some way to the subject of fathers. A large green crepe paper bow is the eyecatcher.

[1] By Frank Gilbreth.
[2] By Henry B. Biller.
[3] By Edward Streeter.
[4] By William Goldman.

THANKS DAD FOR BELIEVING I WAS SPECIAL EVERY STEP OF THE WAY—— FATHER'S DAY—JUNE 17

—STEPS ALONG THE WAY—

BACKGROUND: Light blue paper.

LETTERING: Large—purple door foil on cut-out white posterboard; small—white plastic.

METHOD & MATERIALS: Attach a large circle of purple door foil, cut with pinking shears, to background. Scrounge a pair of baby shoes, paint gold, and hang at center of circle.

—WHAT'S A FATHER?—

BACKGROUND: Black paper.

LETTERING: Light green on black cut-outs (not shown).

METHOD & MATERIALS: Cut out oversized pastel "checks." Letter bank "printing" uniformly, using a black felt pen. Script is in various colors of felt pens. Payees are those firms or folks who might have received payments from Dear Old Dad for services rendered to his offspring.

—CELEBRATE THE SILVER—

BACKGROUND: White paper.

LETTERING: Silver-on-black cut-outs.

METHOD & MATERIALS: Construct family tree with paper dolls, or have students draw their own impressions in crayon. Connect figures with dotted lines made with black felt pen. The sign in the foreground, to be printed with black felt pen or crayons, reads:

> Blessed is the generation in which
> the old listen to the young; and
> doubly blessed is the generation in
> which the young listen to the old.
>
> —The Talmud

—DAYS OF THY YOUTH—

BACKGROUND: A wide border of yellow paper.

LETTERING: Silver cut-outs or stencils filled in with metallic marker.

METHOD & MATERIALS: A collage of faces and scenes depicting the older generation, or a selected student drawing, is framed with strips of black posterboard.

—ALL OVER THIS LAND—

BACKGROUND: Light blue paper.

LETTERING: Red cut-outs edged with black marker.

METHOD & MATERIALS: Cut wings of eagle in segments out of black construction paper; bow them out slightly as you staple them to the board. Cut head from shiny white paper and glue onto a base of red. Add stars of white construction paper.

This board is most effective in a window, where it can be used in conjunction with a selection of books about the geography and technology of America.

AMERICA
WE READ YOU

—AMERICA, WE READ YOU—

BACKGROUND: White paper.

LETTERING: Light-blue-on-black cut-outs.

METHOD & MATERIALS: Paint an impression of the American flag on the center inside sheet of your local newspaper. (No matter if the white stripes are of newsprint, since reading is the board's theme.) If your board is small, use an 11" x 14" newspaper insert. When paint is dry, staple sheet to several others for easier handling. To hang the "book," first pin a length of styrofoam onto the background to act as a brace under the lower part of the "book." Second, position the open "book" on the board and staple along the center line as far down as possible. Roll the edges and staple the underpages of each side, allowing the painted edges to curl slightly. Add bookmark of gold ribbon. Display with books about America—include magazines and newspapers.

See photo, page 64.

–THE AMERICAN SCENE–

BACKGROUND:	Dark blue and red paper, or an appropriate red, white, and blue print fabric.
LETTERING:	Black cut-outs.
METHOD & MATERIALS:	Cut three stars from posterboard: large—white; medium—blue; small—red.

Use this board design in a window to attract attention to a display of Americana. Select one theme or several. Intersperse relevant books with available items from the past, present, and future. For example: past—Indian artifacts, documents, flags, ship models, hats, kitchen utensils; present—newsmagazines, mobile telephone, joggers' earphones, small kitchen appliances, popular board games; future—student-made spaceship models, toy computer, brain model, futuristic fashion photos.

—A BANG-UP 4TH—

BACKGROUND: Dark blue paper.

LETTERING: White cut-outs and white plastic (for *enjoy*).

METHOD & MATERIALS: Cardboard cylinders, such as those used to package potato chips, are used to form firecrackers. Punch holes in the closed end of the cylinders; make each opening large enough to accommodate a fuse of giant-sized yellow or white yarn. Cover cylinders with red paper. Insert fuses through punched openings, pull through to open ends of cylinders, and knot. Now pull fuses back through punched openings and arrange each to terminate in the pages of one of the books in a window display. Align the firecrackers over a strip of styrofoam which is pinned to the board. This arrangement will cause the fuses to stand away from the board. Feature books by American writers on American themes.

—REVELATIONARY BOOKS—

BACKGROUND: Gray or light blue paper.

LETTERING: Large—black cut-outs; small—black plastic.

METHOD & MATERIALS: This collage, made with red, white, and blue construction paper, consists of pinwheels (see insert on illustration), medallions, stars, and a rocket, whose core is a cardboard cylinder. Cover this with colored paper before taping a paper cone onto the head and paper streamers at the tail. This is also effective in a window display featuring books relating to the American Revolutionary War.

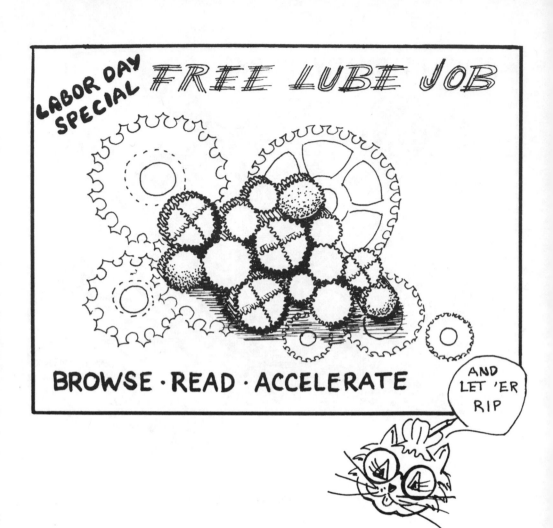

–GEAR UP–

BACKGROUND: Orange paper.

LETTERING: Large—orange-on-black cut-outs; small—black plastic.

METHOD & MATERIALS: Cut large background gears from construction paper in a variety of fall colors. Cut on the fold, as many handicraft books suggest, in order to achieve symmetry. Make smaller gears with corrugated paper (see Hartung, pp. 62-63). This gear arrangement can also be used for Independence Day, under the caption A Declaration of Interdependence.

—LADDER OF SUCCESS—

BACKGROUND: White paper on left two-thirds of board; red and white stripes on remaining one-third (paint white paper or use red crepe paper streamers).

LETTERING: Large—dark blue cut-outs; small—black plastic or cut-outs; subjects—black cut-outs.

METHOD & MATERIALS: The ladder can be made with corrugated paper (a discarded curtain box works well).
Construct as follows:
1. Paint box gold.
2. Cut box in half lengthwise with razor.
3. Shear one 1"-wide strip from each piece to use for criss-cross supports.
4. Remaining sections, cut to 28" length, become sides of ladder.
5. Use leftovers for top and steps.

Assemble the ladder (best held together with straight pins) at the board. Hang objects, such as math tools and art supplies, at the side of the ladder, with giveaway bookmarks in a small bucket. This display is easier to do in a window, where a small stepstool can be used.

See photo, page 65.

—WAITING—

BACKGROUND: Tan burlap.

LETTERING: Large—blue cut-outs; small—white cut-outs.

METHOD & MATERIALS: Director's chairs are put together using two strips of blue denim fabric per chair, cardboard centers of paper towel rolls, and corrugated paper. Tape each end of the wider fabric to cardboard cylinders and roll half-way around cylinders. Pin to board. Staple corrugated strips under chair. Staple narrow denim strips over lower ends of cylinders.

See photo, page 66.

−SCHOOL'S IN−

BACKGROUND: Green paper.

LETTERING: Black cut-outs.

METHOD & MATERIALS: Cut large pickets from white posterboard. Staple each horizontal segment to a styrofoam brace so that the fence will stand away from the board. Perch three plastic, or real, apples on the brace. Cut speech balloon from pale pink posterboard and glue on black letters. Edge balloon with black marker. An appealing picture of a cat or dog peeks through the fence.

—JUDGMENT DAY—

BACKGROUND: White paper.

LETTERING: Black plastic or felt pen.

METHOD & MATERIALS: Using poster paint, or large, colored markers, connote jury with twelve slashes of color, as wide or as narrow as your board can accommodate. The gavel of black posterboard is cut to fit the white circle.

FALL

Armistice Day

Book Week

Columbus Day

Election Day

Halloween

Thanksgiving

United Nations Day

Veterans' Day

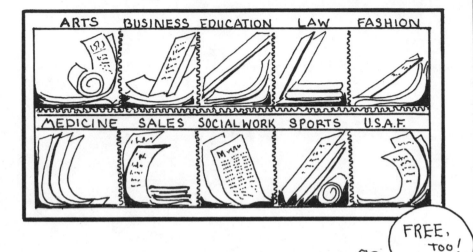

—FALL DELIVERY—

BACKGROUND: Brown wrapping paper.

LETTERING: Large—red, white, and blue stripes; small—black cut-outs or black plastic.

METHOD & MATERIALS: Make mailboxes with corrugated inserts found in boxes used to transport bottles. Attach to board with pins. Label boxes with various career names for which you have a supply of giveaway pamphlets. Replenish boxes frequently as students help themselves.

Include Copycat's comment.

—KNIGHT RIDERS—

BACKGROUND: Green paper, marked with white chalk to suggest playing field.

LETTERING: Two-color cut-outs in your school colors, or copy lettering in illustration.

METHOD & MATERIALS: Fashion football jerseys from construction paper. Print (or cut from white construction paper) statistics for three of your school players on each jersey. Pad shoulders with crumpled newspaper when you pin them to the board. Instructions for a fine helmet, worthy of a true knight, are found in *Card and Cardboard Colorcrafts,* p. 118.

−TIME TO TURN OVER A NEW LEAF−

BACKGROUND: Orange paper.

LETTERING: Tricolored lettering is suggested: glue black letters to red paper, cut again, leaving a ¼" border, then glue to yellow paper and cut once more in the same manner.

METHOD & MATERIALS: Tack real branches to board, using narrow strips of orange background paper. Pin tightly in several spots on either side of the branch. Tack book jackets and pictures, as shown. Staple red florists' leaves at random.

—JUMP NOW—

BACKGROUND:	White paper or fabric.
LETTERING:	Large—black cut-outs; small—black plastic.
METHOD & MATERIALS:	Oversized lettering is bordered by strips of black paper. Jack's trousers and Jill's skirt are cut from construction paper and marked with pen or chalk. Edge the garments in black and sketch feet, legs, and candle. (See Pauli and Mitzit, p. 16, for a 3-D candle made by the catstair method of folding.) Use this board to advertise library activities such as a book fair, sale, or contest. You might also consider using it to call back library books at the end of the school year.

—AN OUNCE OF PREVENTION—

BACKGROUND: White paper.

LETTERING: Large—white cut-outs; small—black plastic.

METHOD & MATERIALS: Paint scaffold with a wide brush and gray poster paint, or build it of gray construction paper torn into strips. Humpty Dumpty is cut from colored construction paper, except for his head, which is of white posterboard edged in black, to effect a contrast between the egg and the white background.

—PURE MAGIC—

BACKGROUND: None.

LETTERING: Black cut-outs.

METHOD & MATERIALS: Tear and arrange large segments of various shades of gray construction paper to approximate shapes of stones in the castle wall. Stipple edges with black magic marker. Cut castle scene from construction paper as follows: light blue sky, yellow sun, gray castle, blue-green water, and three green hills in various shades of green (darkest in foreground). Staple into place. Tack gray paper around castle scene and draw perspective lines with black marker. Shape stones by rounding corners with marker, and stipple to age them.

Include Copycat's comment.

—ROOM TO GROW—

BACKGROUND: Brown paper or fabric.

LETTERING: Various colors of cut-outs.

METHOD & MATERIALS: This easy board is effective in a large window with a broad display of books. Letters should be very large. Make certain the word *grow* curls downward at the edge of the board, giving a cramped effect. This arrangement is the eye-catcher.

–THE TIME HAS COME–

BACKGROUND: Light blue paper.

LETTERING: Blue and green cut-outs.

METHOD & MATERIALS: Use a purchased poster or a drawing of a large walrus. Cut tusks from white posterboard and overlay the poster or drawing with them, for emphasis. Cut stylized surf from white and green construction paper.

–1492 A.D.–

BACKGROUND: Black paper or fabric.

LETTERING: White cut-outs.

METHOD & MATERIALS: Use purchased paper skeletons to depict the Dance of Death, an illustration from the *Nuremberg Chronicle*, the first history of the world, published in 1492. Drape one or two of the skeletons in white crepe paper. Use this board to call attention to a window display, or a collection inside your library, of books about people who lived when Columbus was sailing from Spain. (See Genevieve Foster, *The World of Columbus & Sons*, New York: Scribner, 1965, pp. 170-171.)

—IN MEMORIAM—

BACKGROUND: White paper.

LETTERING: White posterboard cut-outs.

METHOD & MATERIALS: Staple on blue paper to cover the lower third of the board. Cut two hulls from white posterboard; sails are cut in proportion to hulls. Outline all sections with black marker. Divide the duplicate hull in half, placing the prow at board left, and the stern at board right. Try to billow the sails as you staple them in place. Arrange red and yellow flags atop each black mast. The *pièce de résistance* in this display is the lavish application of blue tulle, bunched and pinned here and there over the water area.

See photo, page 67.

—ALL MEN ARE CREATED EQUAL—

BACKGROUND: None necessary.

LETTERING: Black cut-outs.

METHOD & MATERIALS: Construct pole arrangement with black posterboard strips or corrugated paper strips. Affix to stand 1" away from the board, with the help of styrofoam blocks. Hang curtains of tissue paper: pleat double layers and punch near top with hole puncher. Run wire through holes and attach behind the upright poles by winding wire ends around tacks inserted near the top of each pole. Cut clothing, legs, and feet from colored paper. This board would do well in a window, using real poles, fabric, shower rings, and a variety of shoes, i.e., ladies' boots, work shoes, dancing shoes, etc. Make legs of rolled posterboard, placing one end in the shoe, the other behind the clothing.

—ELECTION DAY—

BACKGROUND: Light blue paper, white floor.

LETTERING: Large—dark blue cut-outs; small ("first Tuesday after the first Monday in November")—black plastic.

METHOD & MATERIALS: Uncle Sam's hat (see Wood, p. 96) is very tall, made to sit on the floor of a window display. Red, white, and blue crepe paper streamers emanate from the top of the hat and fly outward. Double each streamer around a large brass ring. Watch newsmagazines and newspapers for write-ups of various candidates' platforms to display on red posterboard. This window is easily adaptable to a board.

—HINDSIGHT—

BACKGROUND: Newspaper. Paint area behind lettering at top with a swath of yellow acrylic or posterboard paint.

LETTERING: Large—white posterboard cut-outs edged with black; small—black cut-outs or black plastic.

METHOD & MATERIALS: Prepare ahead for this board; clip appropriate news items which point up the efficiencies (or otherwise) of local, state, or federal government during the past two or four years. Make clipboards of yellow posterboard, mount news items, and hang, using brightly colored oversized spring clips.

—PROMISES, PROMISES—

BACKGROUND: Pastel paper or fabric.

LETTERING: Large—dark cut-outs; small—felt pen.

METHOD & MATERIALS: Cover circles (records or take-up reels, for example) with white plastic, after first padding them with foam rubber sheets or cotton batting. Pull plastic covering taut and secure at back with tape or rubber bands. Use a variety of lettering styles for each campaign button. (See Ted Hake, *Encyclopedia of Political Buttons, U.S.—1896-1972*, New York, N.Y.: Dafran House, 1974.)

—ABRACADABRA—

BACKGROUND: Left section: tan burlap; center section: orange construction paper; right section: none.

LETTERING: Large—black cut-outs and a variety of colors for *abracadabra*; small—black plastic.

METHOD & MATERIALS: Border your school name with black yarn. Sketch bookshelves with black marker, inserting appropriate Dewey numbers between shelves. Note that the shelves in the left section are angled to achieve a look of depth. Some of this shelving can be carefully stored for reuse in the Library Valentine board (page 110). This board is suitable for a window display. Place the left section on the board itself, and the center and right sections on the window.

—FOUL IS FAIR—

BACKGROUND: Yellow paper.

LETTERING: White cut-outs.

METHOD & MATERIALS: Cut out each segment of this board in triplicate: arrange bodies, flesh-colored hands and faces, black cauldrons over red-and-orange flames, light brown brew, and dark brown stirring handles. Staple tresses of shredded newspaper to each side of the three faces. Hats are lettered as follows: Thane of Glamis, Thane of Cawdor and King of Scotland, the respective salutations of each to Macbeth in the opening act of Shakespeare's play.

—GOTCHA!—

BACKGROUND: Black paper.

LETTERING: White yarn or white cut-outs.

METHOD & MATERIALS: This easy board involves nothing more than a flash-light handle (foil-covered posterboard), a white light ray (cut from freezer wrap), and a round or oval mirror where students will see themselves. It is most effective in a window, with a display of mystery books.

—BOOKS IN A CAVE—

BACKGROUND: Black paper.

LETTERING: White plastic (not shown).

METHOD & MATERIALS: This window display for Halloween can be adapted easily to one dimension. As it is shown, the piñata witch (see Brock, p. 105) and bats (adapt from Drehman, pp. 136 and 116) hang by wire from the ceiling. Cut cardboard to shapes of eyes in illustration. Pad lightly with cotton and cover with white plastic, taping it to cardboard in back. Add large black or purple irises. Display with books on insomnia, mysteries, and other Halloween literature.

—LIFE IN OLD SALEM—

BACKGROUND: Orange paper.

LETTERING: None.

METHOD & MATERIALS: First, determine face area (slightly below center of board); allow room to accommodate cone-shaped witch's hat. (Many papercraft books contain instructions for witches' hats.) Cover entire face area with a collage of news items on Salem wtichcraft (included in jackdaw packet, *Salem Village and the Witch Hysteria*, a mini history course, obtainable from Longman Schools Division, 1560 Broadway, New York, N.Y. 10036). Shred lots of newspaper and tack to either side of face. This hair is most effective—not to mention cheap.

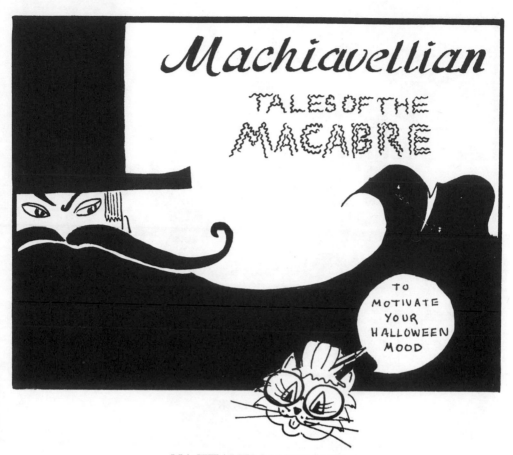

—MACHIAVELLIAN TALES—

BACKGROUND: White paper.

LETTERING: Large—red cut-outs; small—black marker.

METHOD & MATERIALS: Make hat and cape of black construction paper. Mark flesh-colored face with black marker. Add a black yarn handlebar mustache.

—SCARY BOOKS—

BACKGROUND: Brown wrapping paper.

LETTERING: Large—black cut-outs; small—black marker.

METHOD & MATERIALS: Using a black marker, draw two large circles near the top of a large grocery bag. Cut out center of circles. Stuff the bag with crumpled newspaper and pin to board. Decorate board by stapling Halloween candy here and there. In a window display, candy apples can be used along with mystery and horror books.

—VENOM—

BACKGROUND: Black paper.

LETTERING: Large—white cut-outs; small—red plastic and red marker. The five categories are denoted with red plastic lettering, the titles with red marker on a white posterboard base.

METHOD & MATERIALS: This quick and easy board for the Halloween season features book titles of your choice. (Authors of books listed in illustration are, in order of listing: Fletcher Knebel and Charles W. Baily, Emily Brontë, Jay Anson, Robert A. Heinlein, and Jack London.)

—AMERICA THE BOUNTIFUL—

BACKGROUND: Light gray paper.

LETTERING: Gold-on-black cut-outs.

METHOD & MATERIALS: This is a window display for which you should plan well in advance. Gather the following items over a period of time:

Flour bags (good space fillers)—stuff plastic bags with newspaper, tie four corners, and mark with X's.

Oyster or clam shells—display in baskets.

Fruits and vegetables—plastic, raffia, or homemade papier-mâché.

Bread and rolls—real items will work here.

Corn—dried.

Salamis—stuff and tie brown crepe paper rolls.

Eggs—brown plastic.

Hams—stuff cotton bags used to package whole hams (or bags sewn of unbleached muslin) and hang from ceiling.

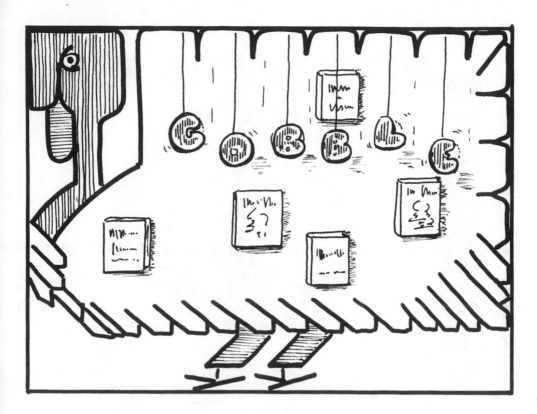

—GOBBLE, GOBBLE, GOBBLE—

BACKGROUND: Tan paper or burlap.

LETTERING: Purple, yellow, and orange cut-outs. Cut three letter forms, one from each color, for each of the six letters in the word *gobble*.

METHOD & MATERIALS: Construct turkey as follows: Cut out head and breast of brown construction paper and wattle of red felt; cut feather segments of various colors of paper. Border all parts with black marker. The feathers form a frame for the open background area, to which are affixed lightweight books or jackets. Staple the three copies of each letter close around a styrofoam ball. Hang these balls from the ceiling of the window display. Make sure all the letters go in the same direction, so that the cry of the turkey is readable as the letters turn.

—A NOVEMBER TO REMEMBER—

BACKGROUND:	Orange paper or fabric.
LETTERING:	Various colors of cut-outs.
METHOD & MATERIALS:	The turkey's body is formed by crushing newspaper to the size you require and wrapping it with masking tape to hold it in shape. Apply colored tailfeathers flat to board. Body feathers, cut from brown construction paper, are glued to the paper shape. Brown felt head and yellow felt feet are attached last. (Instructions for a beautiful turkey are found in Wood, p. 78.)

–READ THEM AND REAP–

BACKGROUND: Tan paper or burlap.

LETTERING: Brown cut-outs.

METHOD & MATERIALS: Construction paper corn,[1] made with green, yellow, and black paper, is arranged in rows. Make each stalk separately, varying sizes. Cut each stalk from one large piece of green construction paper. The leaves should be long and narrow enough to fall away from the board when the stalks are tacked up. Enlargement in left foreground illustrates how to make corn ears: small black construction paper squares are arranged as shown on yellow ears. This is good in a window, where books that elevate the mind and spirit can be displayed on a bed of straw.

---

[1]Construction of corn was conceived by Robert Sutton, a senior at Norview High School, Norfolk, Va., 1983.

Sketches of the Tradition

—SKETCHES OF THE TRADITION—

BACKGROUND: Yellow paper.

LETTERING: Black cut-outs.

METHOD & MATERIALS: Collect art prints depicting Thanksgiving scenes, or send out a call to classroom teachers for student drawings, and frame them with orange construction paper. This board is useful not only at Thanksgiving but at other holiday seasons.

−THANKSGIVING 1750−

BACKGROUND: White paper.

LETTERING: White cut-outs edged with black marker.

METHOD & MATERIALS: Cut figures and all colonial utensils and household items from black construction paper (see D'Amato for ideas).

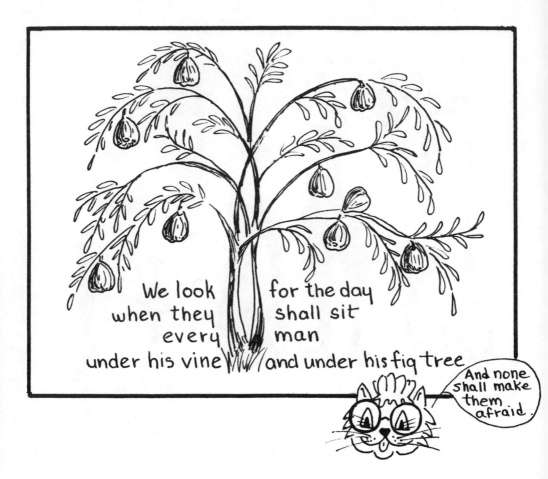

—EVERYMAN—

BACKGROUND: Light green paper.

LETTERING: Several colors of chalk.

METHOD & MATERIALS: Draw the tree directly on the background paper, using brown pastel chalk. Draw leaves with green chalk. Cut figs from tan paper marked with curved strokes of brown and purple chalk. Bible verse is Micah 4:4.

—PEACE—

BACKGROUND: White paper.

LETTERING: Light blue cut-outs.

METHOD & MATERIALS: Try box letters here in 3-D (see Bottomley, p. 78), using box-based children of the world (see Pauli and Mitzit, p. 71). If pressed for time, however, merely hang construction paper hats of different nations on two-dimensional letters.

—TOWN MEETING—

BACKGROUND: Light blue paper.

LETTERING: Black or navy cut-outs.

METHOD & MATERIALS: Lightly trace lines to mark the base of the building and the arc at the top. Construct the United Nations building with strips of white posterboard bordered in black. When stapling strips to board be sure to stay within the lines you have drawn. Add dark blue windows on the three tall pillars. Draw arc and flagstaffs with felt marker and top with colored paper flags. Fringe green construction paper and staple along base of building.

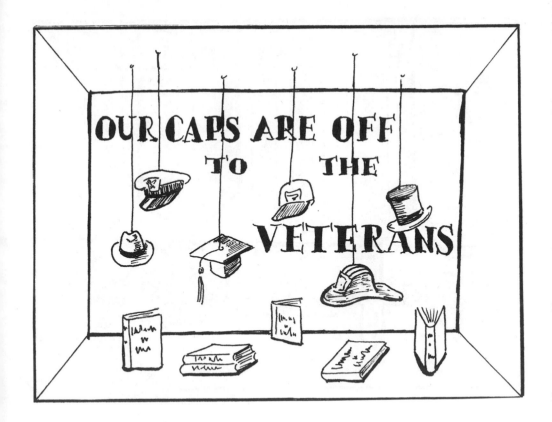

—CAPS OFF!—

BACKGROUND: Light blue paper.

LETTERING: Red cut-outs.

METHOD & MATERIALS: This window display features a variety of hats representing all walks of life, hanging by wire and/or affixed to board with pins. Display with books on wars in which the United States has participated.

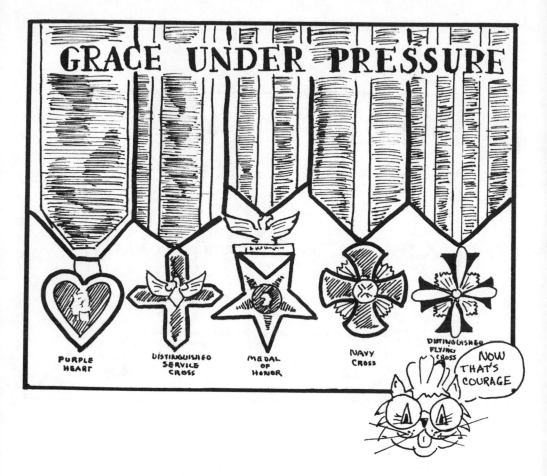

–GRACE UNDER PRESSURE–

BACKGROUND: Light blue paper. This shows only at the bottom of the board, behind the medals.

LETTERING: Large—gold-on-black cut-outs; small—black plastic.

METHOD & MATERIALS: Cut ribbon from construction paper in appropriate colors (see *World Book Encyclopedia*, Decorations and medals). Fashion medals from construction paper and with scraps remaining from gold lettering.

—HONOR THE DAV—

BACKGROUND: None necessary.

LETTERING: Black cut-outs.

METHOD & MATERIALS: Assemble body of truck with gray posterboard, adding red taillights and yellow license plate. Make tires by marking, in the manner of the illustration, gray or white posterboard. Add tire flaps last.

Include Copycat's comment.

—OF THEE WE SING—

BACKGROUND: Light blue paper.

LETTERING: Red cut-outs.

METHOD & MATERIALS: Use a picture or drawing of an eagle or make one with construction paper (see Wood, p. 68). Use posters of representative military figures available from local armed forces recruiting offices and R.O.T.C. Place lettering over stars cut out of white construction paper.

See bulletin board instructions, page 3.

See bulletin board instructions, page 18.

AMERICA, WE READ YOU

See bulletin board instructions, page 23.

See bulletin board instructions, page 24.

See bulletin board instructions, page 37.

STOPPING

BY

WOODS

FROST

See bulletin board instructions, page 80.

See bulletin board instructions, page 87.

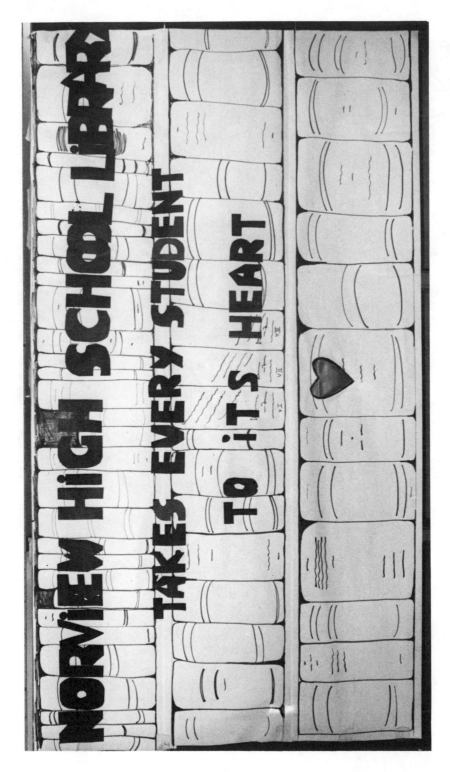

NORVIEW HIGH SCHOOL LIBRARY
TAKES EVERY STUDENT
TO ITS HEART

See bulletin board instructions, page 121.

See bulletin board instructions, page 129.

See bulletin board instructions, page 143.

See bulletin board instructions, page 147.

See bulletin board instructions, page 152.

WINTER

Black History Month

Christmas

Groundhog Day

Hanukah

Lincoln's Birthday

Martin L. King's Birthday

New Years Day

Valentine's Day

Washington's Birthday

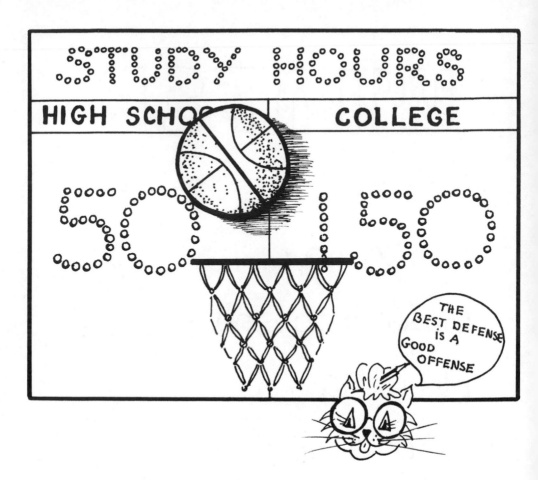

—THE BEST DEFENSE—

BACKGROUND: Black paper.

LETTERING: Large numbers and letters are made with small, uniform circles of yellow paper. White plastic lettering is used for the words *high school* and *college*.

METHOD & MATERIALS: Mark scoreboard lines with white chalk. Draw a net or make one with white cord or yarn as follows: To back side of strapping wire (a thin, narrow steel or plastic band used to reinforce crates or cartons for shipping) tape ends of doubled lengths of cord or yarn at regular intervals. The illustration gives a good idea how to knot the cords. Tack wire to board at either end, bowed out to approximate a half-circle. Make basketball with brown paper, drawing lines with black pen. In a window, hang a basketball piñata (see Brock for ideas) over the white cord net.

–GOOD SERVICE–

BACKGROUND: Top two-thirds of board—gray paper; lower third—cotton batting.

LETTERING: Large—dark blue cut-outs; small—black plastic.

METHOD & MATERIALS: The major requirement for this easy board is a plentiful supply of cotton batting, which is applied over the lower board, on the roof of the building (made of charcoal gray construction paper), and in cloud form, as a base for the small black plastic lettering. Bits of cotton are scattered on upper part of board. Use a real wool cap, or fashion one with construction paper. The flesh-colored hand holds a small book, which is attached to the background by the back cover, using two strips of gray background paper (see Appendix 1 for this procedure).

—THE LAST FLOWER—

BACKGROUND: Light blue or gray paper.

LETTERING: Large—black cut-outs; small—black plastic or felt pen.

METHOD & MATERIALS: Make grass by fringing a mixture of green, tan, and brown construction paper and tack across board at level of base of tree. Sketch tree and leaves with black and brown markers, adding a touch of green to the leaves. Drawings of mouse and hedgehog complete the board. Add black construction paper quills to body of hedgehog and yarn tail to mouse. The 11-line poem is a charming one by John Travis Moore. It is found in the anthology edited by William Cole, *Poems for Seasons and Celebrations* (Cleveland, Oh.: World, 1961), on p. 26.

—REMEMBER THE BIRDS—

BACKGROUND: Gray paper.

LETTERING: None.

METHOD & MATERIALS: Think BIG when you assemble this board. Use corrugated paper, positioned lengthwise and daubed with black marker, to approximate bark. Hang a large onion bag filled with "suet"; make this by wrapping small boxes such as those used to package film. Wrap first in white, then with a double layer of waxed paper. Glue large cotton snowflakes to background in a uniform fashion. The black posterboard limb is laden with cotton, also. Touch up cardinal (cut out from a shiny red cardboard box saved from Christmas) with black markings and a yellow construction paper bill. Pile a dollop of cotton snow on his head.

Include Copycat's comment.

—STOPPING BY WOODS—

BACKGROUND: Cotton batting.

LETTERING: Black plastic.

METHOD & MATERIALS: Mark tan paper tree trunk with black and brown felt markers. Darken color for hole. The raccoon's head, drawn on white posterboard with black and brown markers, is cut out and superimposed over the hole, giving this flat treatment a further dimension. Snow-laden branches of white posterboard are edged with forms of blue-gray paper. Green paper pine needles are added last. Display with books about birds, animals, poetry.

This board was conceived and executed by Robert Sutton, a Norview High School senior in Norfolk, Virginia. This effective board is included to illustrate the wisdom and importance of using talented students in the area of library display.

See photo, page 68.

—BLACK MAGIC—

BACKGROUND: White paper or fabric.

LETTERING: Black cut-outs, sprayed with glue and sprinkled with glitter.

METHOD & MATERIALS: Frame pictures of five black writers. (Inexpensive plexiglass box frames would be handsome here, and can be used in many displays which call for photos, i.e., Native Sons, page 82, A Celebration of Fathers, page 9.) Weave wide black ribbon in and out behind pictures, turning and curling as you go. In a window, allow black ribbon to terminate in pages of the authors' books.

—NATIVE SONS—

BACKGROUND: White paper or fabric.

LETTERING: Large—brown cut-outs; small—black plastic.

METHOD & MATERIALS: The unusual lettering is what will give this display impact: think tall and thin (see Torbet, pp. 196-197). Frame and hang five pictures of black Americans of achievement. Prepare early for this board by writing your request for photos to personages you have selected. Pictures of good quality from magazines will suffice.

Include Copycat's comment.

—STRIDE TOWARD FREEDOM—

BACKGROUND: White paper.

LETTERING: Large—black cut-outs; small—black plastic.

METHOD & MATERIALS: Letter placards with various colors of felt markers and attach to green garden stakes or any clean wood strips you have available. Use small, lightweight boxes for standards. Cover visible sides with white posterboard and letter. They will add variety and depth to the display.

Rum-a-tum-tum

Fa-la-la-la

—CARRYING IN THE BOAR'S HEAD—

BACKGROUND: White paper.

LETTERING: Gold-on-red cut-outs.

METHOD & MATERIALS: Red crepe paper curtains border the display. Mount gold paper horn (horn used in Taps on page 148 will do nicely), white crepe paper baker's hat, and green and black construction paper shoes. The robe is of purple crepe paper trimmed with gold. Tack or staple dark green construction paper stretcher onto background and mark with chalk as shown. Add decorative trim ribbon tacked over tassels of gold felt, each of which is finished with a small bell. With the help of an opaque projector, or a talented student, draw the large boar's head on tan posterboard and cut it out. Cover the cardboard tray with aluminum foil. A red paper apple rests in the boar's mouth. A lot of work and thought is needed for this display, but it will be worth it. If you dare to attempt it in a window in 3-D, see Roth and Bicker, p. 95, for directions for Mr. Piggy.

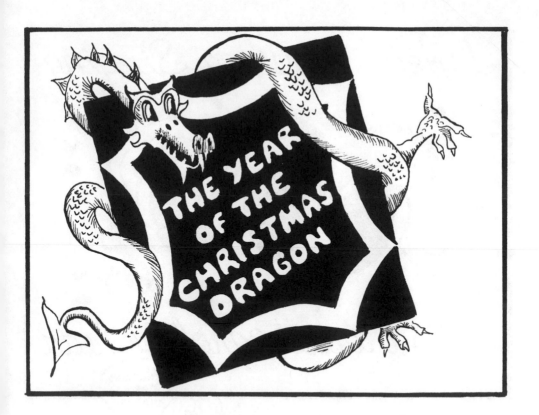

—CHRISTMAS DRAGON—

BACKGROUND: Red paper.

LETTERING: Gold cut-outs.

METHOD & MATERIALS: Use this board to advertise a reading of Ruth Sawyer's *The Year of the Christmas Dragon* (New York, N.Y.: Viking, 1960), to take place in the library. A green dragon is entwined around a rectangle of black posterboard. The dragon can be made with paper by following directions in Wood, p. 72.

–I HEAR AMERICA SINGING–

BACKGROUND: White paper or cotton batting.

LETTERING: Black cut-outs.

METHOD & MATERIALS: Cut three large ovals from black construction paper. Top each mouth with a curved strip of flesh-colored construction paper, drawing faces with felt pen. Add colorful caps, real or made from paper. Musical notes are sketched with black felt marker.

—IT'S FOR YULE—

BACKGROUND: Small figured green-on-white tissue paper.

LETTERING: Large green sparkly garland stapled to background; small—black plastic.

METHOD & MATERIALS: Stuff the bottom half of a shiny white gift box with green tissue, arranging three to five paperback books inside. Add red ribbon and a bright, metallic greeting card. In a window, add wrapped packages, more ribbon, and a selection of Christmas books on a bed of snow.

See photo, page 69.

—MAY YOUR HOLIDAYS BE CHEERY—

BACKGROUND: White cotton batting.

LETTERING: Gold cut-outs.

METHOD & MATERIALS: Determine how much room you will require for lettering before you construct the tree. Next, insert straight pins into the board, first, in a circle, then at strategic points thereafter, downward to the base of the tree: corners of the mouth, the tip of each branch, and corners of the base. Attach a Christmas garland to the end pin in the head area, then wind downward, back and forth around each pin. Your garland should be no wider than one inch, to avoid confusion in the mouth area. Attach lettering with straight pins, then gently pull each letter out from background so that they dangle free.

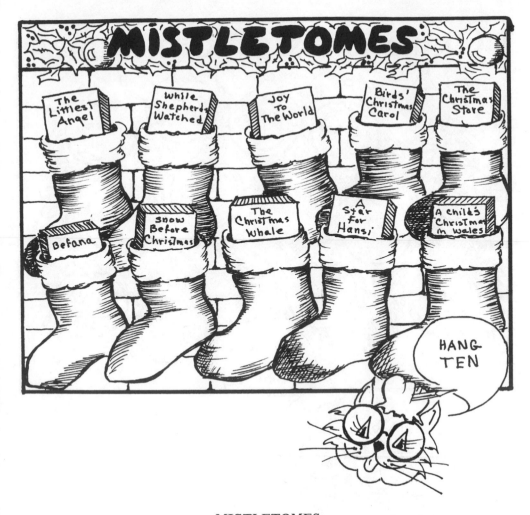

—MISTLETOMES—

BACKGROUND:	Crepe paper with a red brick motif.
LETTERING:	Green cut-outs.
METHOD & MATERIALS:	Use artificial holly to surround the title, which is affixed to a white posterboard mantlepiece. Make or purchase red Christmas stockings, and pin to board as shown. Stuff each one with an appropriate paperback book, or cover small boxes with green paper and add titles in black cut-outs.

—ORNAMENTS OF CHRISTMAS—

BACKGROUND: Green paper.

LETTERING: Red cut-outs or script of red tinsel garland.

METHOD & MATERIALS: Staple purchased imitation greenery (or shredded green tissue paper) over a large portion of the board. Cut hangers from cardboard and cover with foil. Glue them to the tops of ornaments cut from various colors of posterboard. Print names of virtues on ten of the ornaments. Decorate those remaining as lavishly as time and materials allow.

—PAST, PRESENT, AND FUTURE—

BACKGROUND: White paper or fabric overlaid with one layer of green tissue paper.

LETTERING: Script—white ½"-wide yarn; other—2" white plastic letters.

METHOD & MATERIALS: You will need three pictures: Christmas past: a Currier & Ives print or the equivalent; Christmas present: a collage of newspaper headlines and pictures; Christmas future: a reproduction or drawing of The Peaceable Kingdom, by Hicks. Frame each picture with white posterboard. Purchase or make Santa hats.

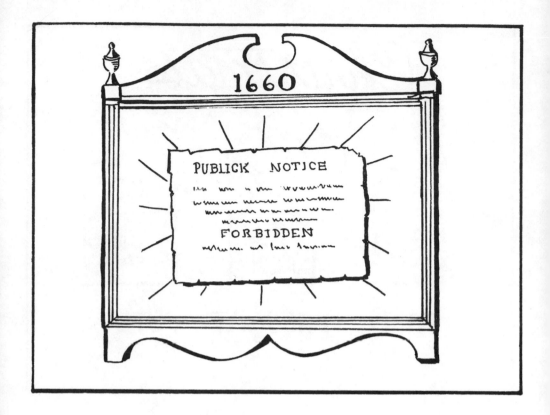

—PUBLICK NOTICE—

BACKGROUND: None necessary.

LETTERING: Numerals in brown cut-outs; notice printed with black felt pen.

METHOD & MATERIALS: Construct tavern sign using black posterboard. Pin taut intersecting lines of black yarn radiating from center of board. Print on brown wrapping paper as follows:

Publick Notice

The obfervation of Christmas having been deemed a sacrilege, the exchanging of Gifts and Greetings, dreffing in Fine Clothing, Feafting and similar Satanic Practices are hereby

FORBIDDEN

with the offender liable to a fine of Five Shillings.

You may want to edge the notice with black marker to give the impression of parchment.

A reproduction of this notice, "Observance of Christmas Forbidden," is available from Buck Hill Association, 129 Garnet Lake Rd., Johnsburg, N.Y. 12843. (Catalog available for $1.00.)

—THREE KINGS—

BACKGROUND: Purple or royal blue door foil.

LETTERING: None.

METHOD & MATERIALS: Fashion crowns (see Wood, pp. 17 and 100) from poster-board. Cover with gold paper or spray-paint. In a window, add unusual objects to hold gold, frankincense, and myrrh. Set each on a bed of straw.

—TO ALL A GOOD BOOK—

BACKGROUND: White paper.

LETTERING: Black cut-outs or black plastic.

METHOD & MATERIALS: Position a large and colorful Christmas book at center of board. Outline lightly with pencil and set aside. Pin together two equal lengths of red and green crepe paper streamers. Stitch along the center of this two-toned streamer a length of red-and-green horsehair braid. This reinforcement will enable you to more easily shape the tree, moving in and out of the pencilled outline and forming a large bow at the base. Mount the book using strips of construction paper, as described in Appendix 1. In a window display, cover the floor with white packing nuggets or white grass and bury interesting titles in the snow.

—HANG IN THERE—

BACKGROUND: Blue-gray sky area.

LETTERING: Black cut-outs (not shown).

METHOD & MATERIALS: Attach corrugated cardboard brown tree trunk, appropriately marked to depict bark. Place a drawing or photograph (enlarged with opaque projector) of a woodchuck near the tree base. Cover the lower one-third of the board with cotton batting, bunched here and there to give an appearance of piled-up snow. Dot the sky area with cotton bits.

—JUST SPRING—

BACKGROUND: Light brown paper.

LETTERING: Large—purple cut-outs; small—black plastic.

METHOD & MATERIALS: Use (or reuse) the snow-covered branches from Stopping by Woods board on page 80. Sketch large black groundhog hole with marker or paint, or cut it out from black construction paper.

Cut groundhog's back and tail from brown construction paper. A furry look is achieved using a fold-and-cut technique (see Grater, *Paper Play,* pp. 103-106 and 203, for examples). Staple cut piece to a duplicate shape and curl all cuts upward.

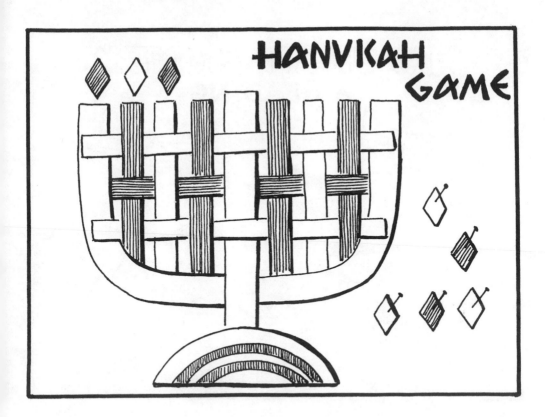

—HANUKAH GAME—

BACKGROUND: Dark green paper.

LETTERING: Yellow cut-outs.

METHOD & MATERIALS: Make the Hanukah lamp of gold and light purple paper or felt. Withhold "flames" to use for playing "Pin the shammash on the Hanukah lamp," a game patterned after "Pin the tail on the donkey." Youngsters can play the game during a library or classroom session in which they are taught about the meaning of this holiday. For complete instructions for game as well as construction of lamp, see Rockland, pp. 133-135.

—HANUKAH MONEY—

BACKGROUND: Dark green paper.

LETTERING: Large—red cut-outs; small—black plastic.

METHOD & MATERIALS: Attach a flesh-colored forearm and hand (made of construction paper) holding a silver tray (made from a foil baking pan). Encase this arm in a full, red sleeve, cut from construction paper with black marker to indicate folds. Cascade play-money bills and coins (see Chaikin, p. 65) across and down the board. Use the display to draw attention to a special December literary event: a reading of Sholem Aleichem's *Hanukah Money* (New York: N.Y.: Greenwillow, 1978).

—HAPPY HANUKAH—

BACKGROUND: Dark green paper.

LETTERING: Silver cut-outs (see Fisher, pp. 46-47, for Hebrew lettering).

METHOD & MATERIALS: This is an easy board to use alone or as a background in a window display. Feature books on Jewish history and handmade Old Testament symbols, i.e., a menorah, tau cross, censer. Consult Rockland for some good ideas.

—THE WESTERN WALL—

BACKGROUND: Brown wrapping paper.

LETTERING: Black cut-outs.

METHOD & MATERIALS: Using a black marker, sketch large stones on background paper. Cut three primitive figures from black construction paper. On oval, flesh-colored heads sketch yarmulkes. Attach sideburns made with black yarn.

The Western, or Wailing Wall, a granitic remnant of Solomon's temple, has been for 20 centuries a place where Jews gather to pray.

Include Copycat's comment in black plastic letters across bottom of board.

—I'VE BEEN TO THE MOUNTAINTOP—

BACKGROUND: Blue paper.

LETTERING: Large—black cut-outs; small—black plastic.

METHOD & MATERIALS: Make mountains with torn (not cut) sheets of dark brown construction paper. Top summits of background mountains with cotton batting. Glue picture of Dr. Martin Luther King to mountain in foreground. Next, staple mountain, bowed slightly outward, to board. Crown this mountain with angel hair, and lace with red sparkle, to simulate fire.

—MANY HAPPY RETURNS—

BACKGROUND: White paper or fabric.

LETTERING: Large—light blue construction paper strips; small—red or black plastic.

METHOD & MATERIALS: Apply lettering to board. Twist bits of red and gold sparkle garland together to serve as flames for the candles. Pin one flame above each vertical line. At center of board assemble a collage of pictures, collected from magazines, of black men, women, and children at work and play.

MARTIN LUTHER KING
1929-1968

1955 - Montgomery, Ala. - Blacks boycott

1963 - Washington, D.C. - Dr. King leads

1964 Stockholm, Sweden - King awarded

1965 - Selma, Ala. - Dr. King leads

1968 - Memphis, Tenn. - Dr. King assassinated

MAY HIS SPIRIT LIVE ON FOREVER

—THE SPIRIT OF LIFE—

BACKGROUND: Old newspaper (avoid headlines and pictures).

LETTERING: Large—black-on-red cut-outs; small—black stencil.

METHOD & MATERIALS: Create newspaper headlines, using stencil forms and black marker.

Include Copycat's comment, written across the bottom of the board with a red marker.

—LINCOLN THEATRE—

BACKGROUND: Lower area—yellow paper; marquee—white posterboard.

LETTERING: Large—black cut-outs; small—black plastic.

METHOD & MATERIALS: Sketch faint lines on marquee to determine placement of lettering. Cut letters to fit and glue in place before mounting on bulletin board. Cut lights from yellow posterboard (note semicircles under marquee); spray with glue and add glitter. Fill lower area with materials on Lincoln: books, pictures, news items, etc., related to the man and his times.

—THE OTHER BIRTHDAY BOY—

BACKGROUND: Black paper.

LETTERING: Black-on-tan cut-outs.

METHOD & MATERIALS: Using straightedge and white chalk, draw a grid of squares on background paper. You will need large pictures of Washington and Lincoln to cut up and patch together in a composite face. Use recognizable features of both men, for example: Washington's hair and nose, Lincoln's eyes and chin. Students will see Washington and Lincoln, but not the other birthday boy; William Henry Harrison (born Feburary 9, 1773). It is hoped they will seek the answer in the library. This board can also be used for Washington's birthday.

—OUR 16TH PRESIDENT—

BACKGROUND: Dark brown paper.

LETTERING: Cut-outs from plaid or striped giftwrap paper, in colors coordinating with the background. Glue letters over a white construction paper base and cut paper to letter shapes, allowing a ¼" border around patterned paper. Script in white yarn.

METHOD & MATERIALS: You will need pictures of presidents who wore beards: Lincoln, Grant, Jackson, Cleveland, Arthur, and Garfield, to do this board. Mat pictures in same color as figures in cut-outs.

—THE COUNTDOWN BEGINS—

BACKGROUND: White paper or fabric.

LETTERING: Black cut-outs.

METHOD & MATERIALS: Cut a semicircle from gray posterboard. Mark minute and hour lines with black marker. Make hands with red construction paper. A quick and easy board, useful in September also.

Include Copycat's comment.

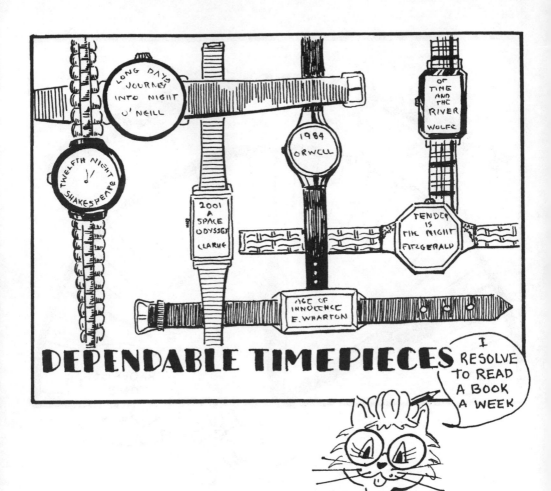

—DEPENDABLE TIMEPIECES—

BACKGROUND: Gray paper or fabric.

LETTERING: Black felt pen.

METHOD & MATERIALS: Use a variety of colors and designs for watchbands, to be made with paper or fabric. Encircle white poster-board watch faces with gold braid or edge with felt pens in coordinating colors. Print on each the titles of books you personally believe to be worthwhile reading.

THIS YEAR EVOLVE INTO SOMETHING BEAUTIFUL

1984 · 1984 · 1984 · 1984 · 1984 · 1984 · 1984 · 1984

—EVOLUTION—

BACKGROUND: Yellow paper.

LETTERING: Large—purple cut-outs; small—black plastic numerals or fine black marker.

METHOD & MATERIALS: Make your butterfly as beautiful as you, or a talented student, can. Consider using a kite, should the size of your board allow. Consult papercraft books for ideas. One very easy method can be found in Wood, p. 30.

The butterfly can be saved to use in an Easter display as a resurrection symbol.

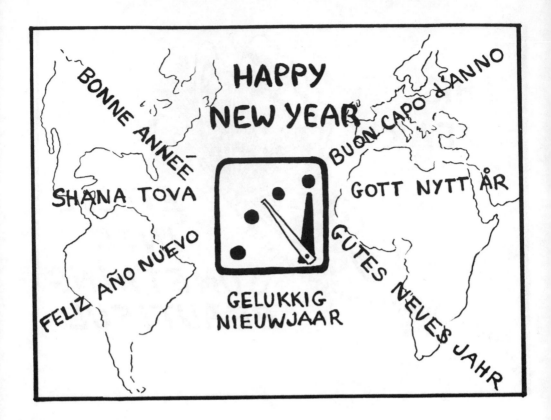

–HAPPY NEW YEAR–

BACKGROUND: Discardable maps, or pastel forms of the continents, applied to a white background.

LETTERING: Large–black cut-outs; small–black felt marker.

METHOD & MATERIALS: Cut continents from discardable maps, or cut pastel construction paper into forms of continents. Make clock bold and colorful, using navy blue paper border around face of white posterboard; glue red paper dots and hands of black and yellow to surface. Boldly letter holiday greetings from around the world.

—THE NEW YEAR AND YOU—

BACKGROUND: Light green paper or fabric.

LETTERING: Pink-on-dark-green cut-outs.

METHOD & MATERIALS: Staple narrow strips of dark green construction paper to serve as background for theatrical masks of comedy and tragedy. Cut out shadow masks of red construction paper. Superimpose on these more elaborate masks cut from posterboard and covered with pink giftwrap. Clip giftwrap so as to facilitate turning it through to rear of mask, where it is to be taped down. Tape red foil behind openings for mouth, eyes, etc. Add red ribbon streamers.

—TEMPUS FUGIT—

BACKGROUND: Provincial print fabric or wallpaper.

LETTERING: Black felt pen.

METHOD & MATERIALS: Cut timer framework from black posterboard and the center glass area from white (outline this section with black marker). Graduate size of lettering from large to small (at neck of timer), increasing again to large as you progress downward. Connote sand with marking pen. If your board is large, or in a window, you might consider making three timers, signifying Education, Maturation, and Graduation, respectively.

—TEXAS CAVIAR—

BACKGROUND: Red and white checked paper or cloth.

LETTERING: Script—narrow rope; other—2" black plastic.

METHOD & MATERIALS: This board is most effective in a window display. The real items will draw students like a magnet. Items in illustration include: decorative wine bottle and cookbook elevated on a box draped with checked background paper; bean pot (partially filled with paper) overflowing with black-eyed peas; small basket holding a white napkin, with onions and garlic nestled in folds; wood-cutting board and knife (slice one onion); pepper grinder; cruet (partially filled with water and drops of yellow food coloring). Type and display a recipe (or two) that includes black-eyed peas.

—A TIME FRAME—

BACKGROUND: Brown wallpaper or wrapping paper in a striped or small-figured pattern.

LETTERING: Brown or black cut-outs.

METHOD & MATERIALS: Cut clock face from posterboard whose color coordinates with pattern in background. With felt marker, boldly designate Roman numerals. On white construction paper print or type titles of books that have won the Newbery or Caldecott award (see Appendix 2 for Newbery and Caldecott award books). At center place a circle of gold, cut out with pinking shears, and labeled with the name of the award whose books are featured.

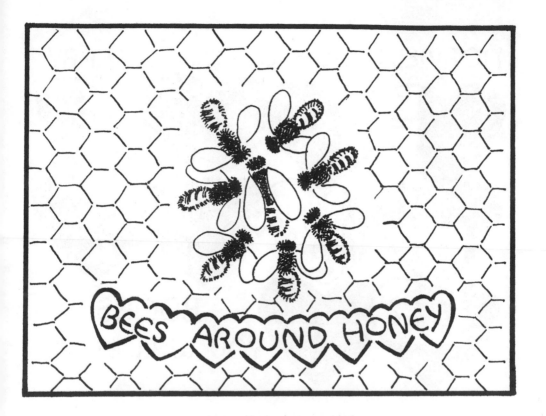

—BEES AROUND HONEY—

BACKGROUND:

Chicken wire, affixed to stand ½" away from board. Pin small blocks of styrofoam at corners and at several other strategic spots around board. Staple chicken wire to these blocks in segments; a single sheet will be too heavy and unwieldy.

LETTERING:

White plastic over red and pink paper hearts.

METHOD & MATERIALS:

Stuff yellow tissue paper into openings in chicken wire at center of board to form a round glob of honey. Make bees with pompons; large yellow ones for bodies, small black ones for heads. Add wings of white wired chenille, called "bumps," available at many craft shops. (Or see Amidon, p. 94, for illustration of quilled bee in 3-D.)

Display books on the subject of love and romance.

—BOOKS YOU WILL LOVE—

BACKGROUND: White paper.

LETTERING: Black cut-outs.

METHOD & MATERIALS: Cut out chains of large red paper hearts—as many as necessary to fill your board. Cut out book jacket covers, or book advertisements, in the same heart shape to cover some of these hearts. Note that some pictures are cut to extend into the row above or below. Of necessity, parts of the jackets or advertisements will be cut out. Retain as much information as possible about the books you are promoting. The heart shapes should be large enough so that your pictures will be decipherable.

—DON'T GET MARRIED—

BACKGROUND: Red construction paper under pink tissue.

LETTERING: Large—shiny red cut-outs (Christmas boxes are a good source for these); small—*very* small black plastic or cut-outs.

METHOD & MATERIALS: Create an opulent, oversized valentine of pink giftwrap, lots of lace doilies (see Ives, p. 85), ribbons, flowers, and gold trim. Display with titles on love and marriage, family life education, divorce, budgets, etc.

—GOIN' STEADY—

BACKGROUND: Blue denim fabric.

LETTERING: Red yarn script.

METHOD & MATERIALS: Using blue denim, sew by hand or machine (with red thread) two hip pockets, each large enough to accommodate a paperback book. Other examples of book pairings are: study—good grades; practice—success; reading—wisdom; exercise—good health.

—HEART'S CONTENT—

BACKGROUND: Red paper or fabric.

LETTERING: White cut-outs or plastic; gold cut-outs for "heart's content."

METHOD & MATERIALS: Make pink satin heart: staple cotton batting to cardboard heart shape, and cover with pink satin fabric. Edge with white lace glued to back of heart. Arrange wide white satin ribbon, such as that used by florists for weddings, as shown. Add handmade or purchased gold letters.

—HEART'S DESIRE—

BACKGROUND: Purple construction paper.

LETTERING: White cut-outs or white plastic.

METHOD & MATERIALS: Using soft pastel chalk—pink, red, or a combination—draw hearts over presketched lines and write in career names. Spray with fixative. In a window, add pertinent material, such as a stethoscope for medicine.

—LIBRARY VALENTINE—

BACKGROUND: White shelf paper.

LETTERING: Black cut-outs.

METHOD & MATERIALS: Sketch bookshelves and books on background with black felt marker. Cut out a heart-shaped opening at bottom row center and edge with black marker. Glue a piece of padded shiny red satin behind the opening. For easy handling, prepare the shelves in three segments before mounting. Attach to board one at a time.

See photo, page 70.

—LOVE'S LABOUR'S LOST—

BACKGROUND: Gray or red paper or fabric.

LETTERING: Black cut-outs (use scraps left from heart[s]).

METHOD & MATERIALS: Black soutache braid serves as a frame for broken heart cut from black posterboard, slashed down the center with a jagged line. Daub irregular edges with white ink or paint to make them stand out. Affix to stand about ½" away from board by gluing to styrofoam or corrugated cardboard strips. This base must be placed close to edges of heart, so that pins can be inserted with ease. You may want to cut another heart of the same size out of black construction paper and place it one inch up and to the left of center, to act as a shadow for the broken heart. (See The New Year and You, p. 111, for illustration of similar treatment). Display with books on alcoholism, child abuse, divorce, prisons, etc. Include books which point to ways out of these predicaments.

—A SIGN OF LOVE—

BACKGROUND: Decorative wallpaper—preferably a green leaf print, but in any case neither too small nor too splashy a print.

LETTERING: Dark green felt pen.

METHOD & MATERIALS: The work of a calligraphy student would add immeasurably to the appearance of this display. If no calligrapher is available, the use of a precut stencil is advised. Trace letters on white posterboard and color with felt pen. Edge the poster with green and black before tacking to board.

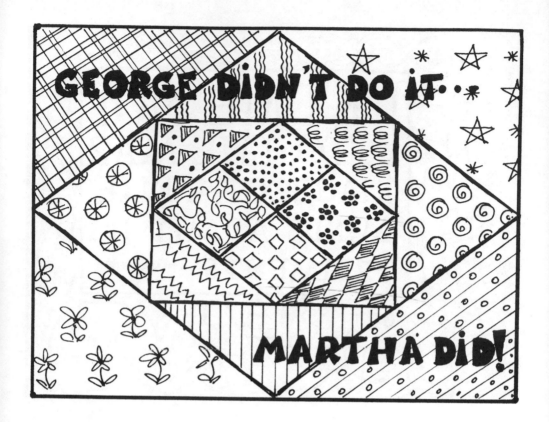

—GEORGE DIDN'T DO IT—

BACKGROUND: Patchwork quilt made from fabric or decorated wrapping paper.

LETTERING: Black cut-outs or black plastic.

METHOD & MATERIALS: Use this board as a come-on for advertising a special collection in your library of books about daily life in eighteenth-century America, in honor of George Washington's birthday. This would be very nice in a window, where artifacts such as documents, kitchen utensils, needlework, money, and weapons can be displayed.

—LET'S BE HONEST—

BACKGROUND: White paper, or fabric with a cherry motif.

LETTERING: Black cut-outs and/or black plastic.

METHOD & MATERIALS: Hang a large, framed portrait of George Washington. If a solid white background is used, decorate with bunches of cherries.

—MOMENT OF TRUTH—

BACKGROUND: Light blue paper.

LETTERING: Black cut-outs.

METHOD & MATERIALS: Cut construction paper segments, enlarging illustration with opaque projector, if necessary:

      Child's clothing—bright colors
      Child's hat and shoes—black
      Breeches—gray
      Stocking—white
      Shoes—black
      Stump—brown and tan (see Fabri, p. 143)
      Hatchet—shades of gray (see Fabri, p. 143)

Add child's features with magic markers.

SPRING

April Fools' Day

Arbor Day

Easter

May Day

Memorial Day

Mother's Day

National Library Week

St. Patrick's Day

—DANCE INTO SPRING—

BACKGROUND: Pink paper.

LETTERING: Dark green cut-outs.

METHOD & MATERIALS: Cut leg and foot shape from light brown posterboard. Cover tightly with white stocking material, taping at back. Wrap a length of white satin ribbon at the ankle as shown. Cut a slipper shape out of cardboard. Pad by gluing cotton batting over cardboard and cover with a scrap of white (or black) satin fabric; tape at back. Hold in place with pins. Gather white tulle and attach at top of board. A corrugated white border trim is the final step. Feature books that are calculated to lift the spirits and overcome the winter doldrums.

–IT'S SPRING AGAIN–

BACKGROUND: White paper.

LETTERING: Yellow yarn.

METHOD & MATERIALS: Make frog in several segments: cut out posterboard shapes and cover with green felt or fabric. His black eyes cut out separately, are lidded in green; the lower rims are lined with white chalk. Glue to head as illustrated. Sketch mouth with black marker. Complete frog with cheeks of pink. Place a bamboo pole (garden stake will suffice) in one or both of the frog's hands. The hurdle is made with strips of construction paper and the crossbar striped with white chalk.

See photo, page 71.

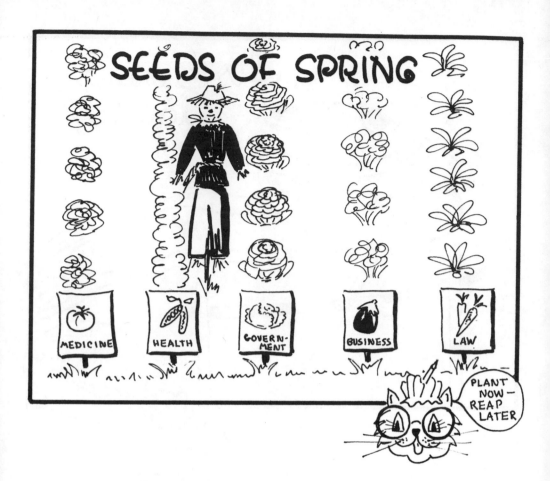

—SEEDS OF SPRING—

BACKGROUND: Brown wrapping paper.

LETTERING: Yellow-on-black cut-outs.

METHOD & MATERIALS: Plant rows with clumps of Easter grass, shaped green tissue paper, and shapes cut from green construction paper. Draw scarecrow between the rows. Draw seed packets on sticks, illustrated with pictures of vegetables and labeled with names of career areas.

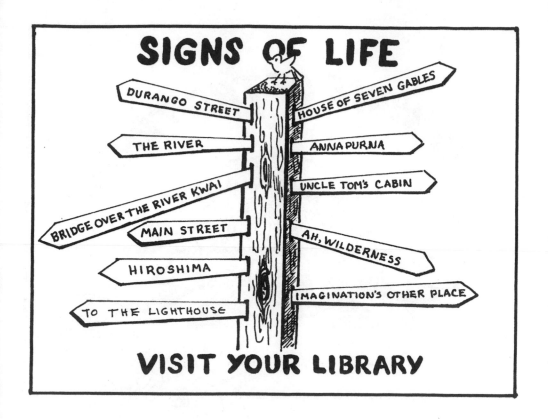

–SIGNS OF LIFE–

BACKGROUND: Light blue paper.

LETTERING: Dark green cut-outs.

METHOD & MATERIALS: Cut signpost from light brown posterboard; draw wood grain with black pen. Draw red bird perched atop post. Cut arrows from a variety of pastel colors of posterboard. Add book titles that include place names with black marker.

—THE VOICE OF THE TURTLE—

BACKGROUND: Yellow paper.

LETTERING: Green cut-outs.

METHOD & MATERIALS: Cut shell of turtle from brown posterboard. Segments of the shell are drawn with pen or quilled (see Bottomley, p. 16), using green yarn. Legs, tail, neck, and head can be done in a cut surface treatment (see Grater, p. 114), or simply drawn, using black marker.

                                        Include Copycat's comment.

—DON'T BE AN APRIL FOOL—

BACKGROUND: White paper.

LETTERING: Large—yellow-on-green cut-outs; script—black marker.

METHOD & MATERIALS: Use a black marker to draw each question mark on a separate piece of white posterboard, after determining the number of squares you will need to fill your board. Align in tight formation. In lieu of Copycat, use an appealing animal picture or drawing.

—FOOLS RUSH IN—

BACKGROUND: Red brick-patterned crepe paper or other decorative paper with a brick or stone wall motif.

LETTERING: Black cut-outs.

METHOD & MATERIALS: A quick and easy board for April Fool's Day.
Include Copycat's comment.

—WE WOULDN'T FOOL YOU—

BACKGROUND: Light blue paper or fabric.

LETTERING: Script—bright blue yarn; other—blue marker.

METHOD & MATERIALS: On light blue posterboard print, "The library—you can't find better books if you stand on your head" with dark blue marker and affix upside down to bottom of board. Attach real or hand-drawn book jackets on lightweight boxes for a 3-D effect and pin onto board upside down.

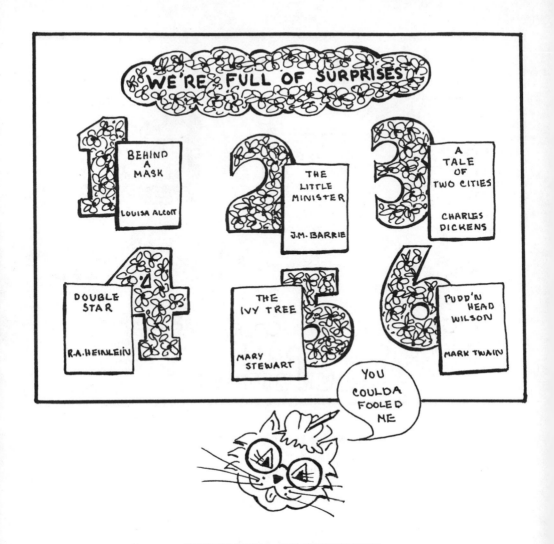

—WE'RE FULL OF SURPRISES—

BACKGROUND: Yellow paper.

LETTERING: Black plastic on flowered contact paper; large numbers are cut out from same paper.

METHOD & MATERIALS: Using pastel chalk or felt pen, design and label your own book covers on purple construction paper. Use titles which deal with individuals who assume or act the character of another person, such as: *Behind a Mask* (Louisa May Alcott), *The Little Minister* (J. M. Barrie), *A Tale of Two Cities* (Charles Dickens), *Double Star* (R. A. Heinlein), *The Ivy Tree* (Mary Stewart), *Puddn'head Wilson* (Mark Twain). For further titles, consult H. W. Wilson Company's Fiction Catalog.

—APPLES ON A STICK—

BACKGROUND: Light green paper.

LETTERING: Large—a combination of short lengths of green garden stakes and dark green paper; small—light-green-on-dark-green cut-outs.

METHOD & MATERIALS: Insert stakes into styrofoam balls. Cover each ball with red cellophane and tie with white paper ribbon. Add remaining letters of dark green paper. This display is most effective in a window, where you can display books and items associated with this folk hero, i.e., a backpack, burlap sack, old cooking pan, and a bevy of small stuffed animals.

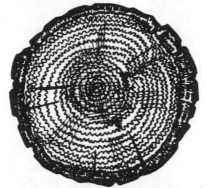

like a tree . . .

. . . your library is a diary
that everyone can read

—TREE OF LIFE—

BACKGROUND: None if board is tan; otherwise, tan paper.

LETTERING: Yellow-on-black cut-outs.

METHOD & MATERIALS: Take a few days, at odd moments, to assemble this board. The process of creating it will arouse curiosity among the students. Use ¾"-wide corrugated paper strips for tree cross section. You will need a large supply of long pins (1"). Insert pins through openings of corrugated paper into the board at short intervals.

First, make the pith by winding a couple of strips in a tight spiral. Second, determine the *outer* line of the heartwood area (midway between bark and pith), and then pin strips, starting at that outer circle; work inward, round and round, to meet the pith area. The formation here need not be tight. Third, wind paper more tightly for the lesser sapwood area. Fourth, add the bark, using 1½"-wide corrugated paper strips folded lengthwise (brace on a counter edge to fold easily). Pin bark, folded end up (openings against board), by inserting pins diagonally at the base through to the board. Fifth, paint the pith and sapwood areas yellow and the heartwood black, using poster or acrylic paint.

A representation of this cross-section measuring 27" x 25" requires about 50 yards of ¾" strips and 2½ yards of the folded bark layer.

—AN EGGSTRAORDINARY EASTER—

BACKGROUND: White or pink paper.

LETTERING: Black cut-outs or black plastic.

METHOD & MATERIALS: The basket is constructed of a lightweight box (15"L x 10"W x 5"D for 48"-square bulletin board). Cut away one long side of box. Make 1"-2" cuts at the base opening on each side. This will allow you to fold sides and bottom inward, forming tabs which allow you to tack basket to board. Decorate first, however, by weaving strips of yellow and green crepe paper over front and sides, leaving the tabs free. Hold crepe paper in place with glue and a few staples. The handle and basket border is made by twisting wide strips of dark green crepe paper and thick white yarn together around a length of strapping wire. Attach trim to basket with staples and pins. At lower board, securely pin a length of styrofoam. Set basket on this brace and hold to board by tacking along tabs you made earlier. Fill basket first with crumpled tissue paper, then with selected paperbacks or facsimiles. Hold in place with paper strips (see Appendix 1). Tuck bunny or chick among books and fill open areas with purchased Easter grass. Attach handle with pins and add a large yellow crepe paper bow.

Include Copycat's comment.

—HISTORY IN A BASKET—

BACKGROUND: Apply purple squares over a yellow background in a checkerboard effect.

LETTERING: Black cut-outs.

METHOD & MATERIALS: Collect a variety of baskets and hang them by wires, affix them to board, and place them on the floor of a window. Use real baskets, or make them. See Eckstein, p. 114, for covered berry baskets, and Wood, p. 106-111, for baskets of paper. Fill each basket with Easter grass, adding books selected from your 900 area.

—PEACOCKS AND LILIES—

BACKGROUND: Green paper or fabric.

LETTERING: Print Ruskin quotation (below) on posterboard and place on or near display.

METHOD & MATERIALS: See Torbet, pp. 55-57, for pattern, simple and full sized, of the peacock, a resurrection symbol. The title is based on John Ruskin's statement: "Remember that the most beautiful things in the world are the most useless; peacocks and lilies, for instance" (*Bartlett's Familiar Quotations*, 14th ed., Boston: Little, Brown, 1968, p. 698b).

—HURRAY, HURRAY—

BACKGROUND: Yellow paper.

LETTERING: Green cut-outs.

METHOD & MATERIALS: Tape three to five paper towel centers (or as many as needed to fill your board) end to end. Cover with green tissue paper. Starting at the top, attach pink paper ribbon at an angle. Wind downward attaching with a dab of glue every few inches. Attach pink crepe paper streamers at the top and pin to look as if flying outward.

Draw butterflies here and there. Paper or plastic flowers decorate top of maypole, along with a styrofoam ball covered with gold foil.

—PUSHIN' UP DAISIES—

BACKGROUND: Light blue paper and green imitation grass on lower half.

LETTERING: Yellow-on-white cut-outs.

METHOD & MATERIALS: This May board is a reminder for students to get books back to the library before the close of the school year. Superimpose inexpensive white fencing over background. Hold to board with rolled pieces of masking tape, sticky side out, attached to back of slats and then pressed to board. Draw in butterflies (see Eckstein, p. 29, for cut-out version). Fill vases and/or baskets with paper daisies and place them on the circulation desk. (Many flower-making books contain daisies. For a pattern and instructions for a cartridge paper daisy, see Ives, pp. 66-69.) A student who returns his or her book(s) is privileged to sign a flower and "plant" it. The object, of course, is to fill the board with a field of daisies.

Include Copycat's comment.

See photo, page 72.

—SPRINGTIME IN THE KREMLIN—

BACKGROUND: Red paper.

LETTERING: Script—black marker; other—black cut-outs or black plastic.

METHOD & MATERIALS: Cut hammer and sickle from yellow posterboard. Identical, goose-stepping soldiers are cut from newspaper. Diminish in size, however, as rows approach top of board.

Include Copycat's comment, from Bertrand Russell, *Unpopular Essays* (New York: Simon and Schuster, 1950), p. 106: "Fear is the main source of superstition, and one of the main sources of cruelty. To conquer fear is the beginning of wisdom."

—HANG IT UP—

BACKGROUND: Black paper or fabric.

LETTERING: Red plastic or red cut-outs.

METHOD & MATERIALS: Make several newspaper hats (see Eisner and Weiss, p. 65). Hang from long pins in a row, close together, as if in a closet. Borrow, or purchase, toy rifles and hang one beneath each hat.

—OLD SOLDIERS—

BACKGROUND:	Brown wrapping paper.
LETTERING:	Large—black cut-outs; script—black felt marker.
METHOD & MATERIALS:	Cover five to seven posterboard rectangles with camouflage fabric. Add military book titles in colored marker, and perhaps pictures you have on hand of authors and war scenes. The books disappear in a cloud of black smoke—angel hair sprayed black. In a window, arrange accoutrements of war, along with a book display.

—SOLDIER OF A GREAT WAR—

BACKGROUND: Camouflage fabric or abstract shapes of tan and brown paper.

LETTERING: 1" and 2" black stick-on letters.

METHOD & MATERIALS: You will need five or six sheets of gray posterboard (the reverse side of previously used posterboard is fine). Cut out as many as 30 gravestones, all relative in size to the main headstone, made of a cereal box (a 14" x 10" size works well on a 50" square board). Glue gray posterboard to front of box, with sides and rounded top extending beyond box edges. Apply lettering and staple on a red silk rose. Tear the edges of some of the stones to give the feel of antiquity. Staple background stones to board, with tall, narrow ones at top and short, wide ones at bottom. Affix main headstone with staples and pins. Staple imitation grass at lower edge. If irony is not suitable to your audience, substitute another phrase, such as "Remember Our Soldiers."

See photo, page 73.

—TAPS—

BACKGROUND: White paper (freezer wrap is wide and sturdy).

LETTERING: Black cut-outs.

METHOD & MATERIALS: American flag is made with blue and red construction paper, torn rather than cut to give the impression the flag is blowing in the wind. White stars should be irregular in order to further this effect. Fashion bugle from posterboard and cover with gold paper. Add posters or pictures of World Wars I and II.

–VIETNAM MEMORIAL–

BACKGROUND: Gray posterboard.

LETTERING: Black felt pen.

METHOD & MATERIALS: Draw light guidelines on posterboard. Print names[1], row upon row, as in illustration. Add black silhouette in foreground and a real flag to complete the board. (Enlarge and trace silhoutte in illustration, using an opaque projector, or seek a talented student's help.)

[1] Selected names from the Vietnam Memorial follow: Douglas H. Leach; Robert L. Lewis; Roy Lockhart; William B. Mitchell; Samuel L. McDonald; Charles V. McManus; Carl I. Palmer; Donnell Phillips; Floyd L. Reed, Jr.; Robert L. Stokes; William T. Victory; Ivory Ward, Jr.; Benedicto P. Bayron; Dale R. Buis; Ralph W. Magee; Bruce R. Jones; John R. Ackerman; Michael C. Delacy; Danny E. Carlton; Ruben G. Chavez; Donald C. Cornett; John R. Urban; Robert J. Betz; Tommy Keeton. Inscription to right of date reads: "In honor of the men and women of the armed forces of the United States who served in the Vietnam War. The names of those who gave their lives and of those who remain missing are inscribed in the order they were taken from us."

—M IS FOR MOTHER—

BACKGROUND: Light green paper.

LETTERING: Initial M—dark green posterboard cut-out; small—black plastic; script—black soutache braid.

METHOD & MATERIALS: Make mother hen after the manner of a provincial tea cozy: body—yellow provincial print fabric; head and breast—solid red print. Nestle her on a bed of Easter grass and add purchased baby chicks. To achieve the effect of an illuminated manuscript, decorate the initial M with felt markers. Metallic markers are good for highlighting. Interlace vines of light green yarn. (See Appendix 1.) A quilled letter would be effective, also (see Amidon, p. 60).

—MOTHER KNOWS BEST—

BACKGROUND: Yellow paper, trimmed at bottom with green construction paper or crepe paper grass.

LETTERING: Cut-outs of various colors.

METHOD & MATERIALS: Construct shoe with three segments of brown poster-board. Use corrugated paper strips for roof. Pin over-sized yellow yarn shoelace and bow to front of shoe, and mark laceholes with black marker. In a window display, place the mailbox, made of black construction paper, on a wooden post (otherwise, post is brown construction paper). Display with books on family life, or those with titles which include the word *mother*.

who saw ME in all,
and saw all in ME,
For her I am not lost
And she is not lost
for me.

—SHE—

BACKGROUND:	Pink paper.
LETTERING:	Large—white cut-outs edged with black marker; small—purple crayon.
METHOD & MATERIALS:	First, determine size of carriage you will need. Cut out from black posterboard in six segments, plus wheels, struts, and handle, paying close attention to the shape of each part and the positioning of each shape against the other. It is advisable to work out a pattern with newspaper before you begin. The balloons are made by padding ¼" thick cork circles with cotton batting, then covering them in a variety of bright colors of paper. Staple a white yarn string to each. The quotation, printed in crayon, is from the *Bhagavad Gita.* See *Bartlett's Familiar Quotations,* 14th ed. (Boston: Little, Brown, 1968), p. 106b.

See photo, page 74.

—'TWAS EVER THUS—

BACKGROUND: Green paper.

LETTERING: Large—green-on-rust cut-outs; small—black cut-outs or black plastic.

METHOD & MATERIALS: Weave papyrus with torn strips of unbleached muslin. First press strips between two sheets of waxed paper. The melted wax will stiffen the material sufficiently for easier handling. In a window, display books in which mother love is exemplified from different periods of history.

—WE'LL BE GOOD—

BACKGROUND: Top—light blue paper; bottom—blue-green paper.

LETTERING: Dark green cut-outs.

METHOD & MATERIALS: Cut many cream-colored and dark and light brown feathers for mother duck from construction paper. Arrange over crumpled newspaper for a 3-D effect. Apply glue to feathers only at the base. In a mixture of colors (except for the cream-colored underside), tuck one behind the other over the newspaper base until base is completely covered. When dry, attach body to board with pins.

Orange construction paper legs disappear behind blue-green water. Cut out five to seven ducklings in various shades of yellow and mark details with felt pen (or adapt directions for making floating swans in Janvier, p. 18). Cut slits in the water area with a razor and insert ducklings.

—A WOW OF A LADY—

BACKGROUND:	Pink or yellow paper.
LETTERING:	Large—purple cut-outs; small—white plastic or white cut-outs.
METHOD & MATERIALS:	Solicit drawings or written testimonies on the subject "Mother" from students and/or teachers. Set each submission in a purple construction paper frame. Decorate with daisies (see Eckstein et al., p. 26, for paper plate flowers). Use as many items as your board can accommodate.

−CHECKMATE−

BACKGROUND:

White paper. Color or cut red squares into forms that will give the perspective in the illustration.

LETTERING:

Large−black cut-outs; small−black plastic.

METHOD & MATERIALS:

Chessmen can be drawn on the board or made from regular or oversized playing cards (see Carroll, p. 75). Insert each card into a thin balsawood base slit with a razor. (To secure card, apply glue along the narrow opening you have made). Affix by inserting pins diagonally underneath the base. This will allow cards to stand away from board. In a window, continue the background across the floor to the window's edge.

—GO BY THE BOOK—

BACKGROUND: Green plastic leaf bags.

LETTERING: Large G and S—orange and yellow posterboard cut-outs; others—white plastic.

METHOD & MATERIALS: Cover five to seven lightweight boxes, such as cereal and cracker boxes, with scraps of green plastic. Cut orange, yellow, and green posterboard strips to fit one side of each box. Print titles of reference books that are in your library with black marker and glue one spine to each box. Make a strong base (not visible) for boxes: wrap masking tape to three or four spots on a length of styrofoam, the extended ends of which come together to form a tab. Tack, or staple these tabs to board. Next, pin the boxes in a pile. Fill the floor of a window with more green plastic. Display with five to seven reference books and other research materials.

—HOT OFF THE PRESS—

BACKGROUND: Gray paper.

LETTERING: White cut-outs.

METHOD & MATERIALS: Make bookpress with black posterboard. Cut out press parts with paper cutter. Shape finials and other rounded parts of press with a razor. Threads are indicated by gluing on white construction paper rectangles at regular intervals. Letter, in black, on a variety of colored posterboard strips, some new titles in your library.

—HOW TO BE A FAT CAT IN A LEAN YEAR—

BACKGROUND: Top one-third—dark blue paper; lower two-thirds—brown wrapping paper.

LETTERING: Black felt marker.

METHOD & MATERIALS: Draw details of fence boards with black felt pen. Cut out four cats in various colors, mark features with felt pens, set close together on top of the fence. Yellow moon and stars decorate the sky area.

Include Copycat's comment.

—THE MAIN EVENT—

BACKGROUND: Plaid paper or fabric.

LETTERING: Large—cut-outs; small—black plastic.

METHOD & MATERIALS: The appeal of this board, designed to advertise library activities, depends for its success on color and lettering style. The word *event* must be very large in relation to the other words. Pick the lightest and brightest color of the plaid you have selected, and use this shade of construction paper to form the large letters. Dot, as the illustration shows, with a felt-tipped pen.

—GO FOR THE IRISH—

BACKGROUND:　　　　Light green paper.

LETTERING:　　　　Cursive writing—dark green yarn; other—black plastic or cut-outs.

METHOD & MATERIALS:　　Construct traffic light with black posterboard. Red and amber lights are cut from posterboard; green light is depicted with green sparkle garland wound round and round from center to perimeter of circle and affixed with glue. Top with purchased green bowler hat (bisected and held on board with pins). Print names of Irish authors on street signs of various colors.

—THE GREENING OF THE LIBRARY—

BACKGROUND: Light green paper or fabric.

LETTERING: Script—dark green yarn; small—black plastic.

METHOD & MATERIALS: Make green paper hat with wide, black band and shiny gold buckle. Use purchased pipe or make from construction paper. Get this board up early and institute an Annual Limerick Contest, in which entries are read and judged on St. Patrick's Day in the library. Include instructions for participation (The Rhymin' o' the Green), along with samples of famous limericks.

—IRISH BULL—

BACKGROUND: Light green paper.

LETTERING: Script—dark green yarn. Cut capital letters from dark green paper to serve as bases for the beginning letter of each word.

METHOD & MATERIALS: Make a bull mask of papier-mâché, or create with construction paper: head: pink; eyes—green, with long black felt lashes; horns—white. Tack over a large dark green cloverleaf base. Add purchased paper hat if desired. Scatter paper shamrocks on background. Type a sign reading "See *Dictionary of Literary Terms*" and mount on a row of small shamrocks. Display with books of nonsense verse and related subjects.

—THE LAND ACROSS THE BAY—

BACKGROUND: Light green paper.

LETTERING: Dark green cut-outs.

METHOD & MATERIALS: Cut map area from dark green paper, except for Northern Ireland, which is red. Superimpose on this a facsimile of the Muiredach Cross, fashioned from corrugated paper (see Hartung for inspiration).

—LITTLE PEOPLE—

BACKGROUND: White paper.

LETTERING: Dark green cut-outs.

METHOD & MATERIALS: Cut out outline of Ireland using green paper. Staple green Easter grass over entire map area. Pin on finger puppets, trolls, or any "little people" that you can borrow or beg in sufficient number to be noticeable. Scatter paper shamrocks on background.

—APPENDIX 1—
TECHNIQUES FOR CONSTRUCTING BULLETIN BOARDS

BACKGROUNDS

Select your background paper or fabric with care. It is the foundation of your bulletin board and sets the mood for your message. Backgrounds must lie flat and tight against the bulletin board. Hold them with tacks or staples. Suggested paper backgrounds are:

White shelf paper or freezer wrap

Fadeless art paper (available in craft and teacher supply stores)

Paper tablecloths

Construction paper

Brown wrapping paper

Giftwrap

Wallpaper

Foil (wide variety available during Christmas season)

Newsprint (use comic pages for color)

Fabric backgrounds have the advantage of longer wear. If stored with care (rolling is best), fabric can be used repeatedly through the years. Some suggestions are:

Cotton prints:
    animals
    border motifs
    checks
    flowers
    plaids
    polka dots
    provincial

Burlap

Cotton batting

Felt

Memorize or make note of dimensions of board(s) for which you are responsible, so you will know exactly how much fabric to buy when shopping. Accumulate a stockpile of basic colors, such as white, black, light blue, yellow, and red. Seek a variety of textures in each color—white cotton batting, white broadcloth, white burlap, white-on-white damask print, white felt, and so on.

DRAWING

Simple forms like penguins, pilgrims, and maps are best enlarged and outlined with the opaque projector. The grid method (see Torbet, p. 24), although time consuming, is also effective. Children's coloring books are a rich source for simple, easy-to-enlarge patterns. Consider enlisting talented students to participate in drawing projects.

FRAMES

A quick and easy method for making frames is to use patterns. Collect photograph mats in an assortment of sizes (3x5, 5x7, 8x10) and shapes (square, round, oval) to serve this purpose. Determine the best size and shape by trying mats over your picture. Trace the pattern of your choice on construction paper or posterboard and cut out. Posterboard mats can be stenciled, using plastic templates, with cut-outs of various shapes. Fill in with colored markers (see Torbet, p. 76). Other treatments are:

1. Center pictures on textured backgrounds, such as cork or rush rug squares. Allow for a border to frame the picture.

2. Glue pictures to a 1" thick styrofoam base cut to the exact measurement of the picture. Good in a collage.

3. Purchase plexiglass frames of the type that have a glass cover that fits over a box insert. Precut holes allow for hanging either vertically or horizontally. These frames are handsome and can be used for years.

See Wankelman for good instructions for matting and framing pictures.

GRASS

Fringe strips of green tissue or construction paper. Trim to varying lengths. Tack to board, overlapping strips. Layer where more fullness is required.

Purchased grass of the kind manufactured for use in Easter baskets is effective and reuseable. Staple to board in clumps; this grass almost holds itself against the board and requires a minimum of staples.

A purchased grass mat (available in craft and teacher supply stores) is worth the expense for libraries that have window display areas.

HAIR

An effective treatment for simulating hair on a bulletin board is with fringed newspaper. Proceed as follows:

1.   Determine the length of hair needed.

2.   Fold in half a sheet of newspaper that measures twice the required length.

3.   Make continuous cuts ¼" apart along doubled edge of sheet, ending ½" from fold. Cut *through* fold every 1½" to create a lock of hair.

4.   Staple locks to board, clustering around the ear area.

LETTERING

Make your message bold and colorful. See Bielgeleisen for a portfolio of alphabet styles, or Torbet, which features five sample alphabets. Trace and copy some of these alphabets on lightweight cardboard. Cut out, label, and file in manila envelopes for future use.

Cut-out lettering (often used in conjunction with plastic letters) is the easiest and most effective method of lettering on bulletin boards. Proceed as follows:

1.   Determine requisite size.

2.   Cut construction paper squares in required size, one for each letter.

3.   Lightly sketch letter shapes. Cut and trim.

See Wankelman for instructions on cut paper lettering.

Always keep in mind the number of letters in your statement. The shorter the caption, the larger your letters can be. For a long caption, you must reduce letter height to a workable proportion. Remember that some letter forms are necessarily wider than others (M and W, for example) and require more space. To avoid space problems, cut out individual letters at the board. Attach the opening word of your caption first. Next tack in place the last word. Work inward back and forth to the center, making on-the-spot adjustments to assure a proper fit.

When instructions call for one color cut-out letter on another, cut overlay letters ¼" to ½" smaller than base letters. Glue overlay letters to base letters. Staple or glue letters to board.

Pin-back letters and numbers (obtainable from many school supply catalogs) are great timesavers. They also add a professional touch. They are secured with pins but may sometimes require a touch of glue over thick backgrounds like cotton batting.

Yarn or garland script, is pinned to board over lightly sketched lines. See photo, p. 72.

For illuminated manuscript (see M is for Mother, p. 150), proceed as follows:

1.   Draw a simple letter with a clean, flowing line on posterboard or lightweight cardboard. Border the letter with black felt marker.

2.   Decorate with colored and metallic markers.

3. Cut letter out.

4. Interlace vines of green yarn around letter, and pin the whole into place on board.

MOUNTING BOOKS

To mount a book, you need 3 1"-wide strips of background material, of lengths which allow a 1" extension at either end when applied to board as follows:

1. Arrange all strips *under* the front cover and *over* the pages and back cover.

2. Place 2 strips diagonally across the upper and lower right corners. Tack extensions close to cover edges.

3. Place the third strip along spine and tack extensions at upper and lower edges.

4. A bit of rolled masking tape or floral decorator adhesive placed between front cover and first page will prevent cover from falling open.

Obviously, you should only attempt to mount books that are small or lightweight.

Facsimiles of large or heavy books can be made by reproducing simple jacket covers on posterboard, using construction paper and felt markers. Photocopy more complex covers and color with felt pens. Mount finished products on 1"-thich styrofoam base cut to size of book.

When it is necessary either to brace a weighty object or to hold it away from the board, use styrofoam cut to fit under the object without being seen. Affix to board with long pins inserted diagonally at the corners, bottom, and sides. The brace can be made stronger by attaching strips of masking tape at several points along the styrofoam, each one forming tabs extending two or three inches beyond the two back edges. Tack these tabs securely against board.

NEWBERY MEDAL

1984 Cleary. *Dear Mr. Henshaw.* (Morrow).

1983 Voigt. *Dicey's Song.* (Atheneum).

1982 Willard. *A Visit to William Blake's Inn: Poems for Innocent and Experienced Travelers.* (Harcourt).

1981 Paterson. *Jacob Have I Loved.* (Crowell).

1980 Blos. *A Gathering of Days: A New England Girl's Journal, 1830-32.* (Scribner).

1979 Raskin. *The Westing Game.* (Dutton).

1978 Paterson. *Bridge to Terabithia.* (Crowell).

1977 Taylor. *Roll of Thunder, Hear My Cry.* (Dial).

1976 Cooper. *The Grey King.* (McElderry/Atheneum).

1975 Hamilton. *M. C. Higgins, the Great.* (Macmillan).

1974 Fox. *The Slave Dancer.* (Bradbury).

1973 George. *Julie of the Wolves.* (Harper).

1972 O'Brien. *Mrs. Frisby and the Rats of NIMH.* (Atheneum).

1971 Byars. *Summer of the Swans.* (Viking).

1970 Armstrong. *Sounder.* (Harper).

1969 Alexander. *The High King.* (Holt).

1968 Konigsburg. *From the Mixed-Up Files of Mrs. Basil E. Frankweiler.* (Atheneum).

The Newbery is awarded annually for the "most distinguished" text of the preceding year. Dates indicate year of award, not year of publication.

1967   Hunt. *Up a Road Slowly.* (Follett).

1966   Treviño. *I, Juan de Pareja.* (Farrar).

1965   Wojciechowska. *Shadow of a Bull.* (Atheneum).

1964   Neville. *It's Like This, Cat.* (Harper).

1963   L'Engle. *A Wrinkle in Time.* (Farrar).

1962   Speare. *The Bronze Bow.* (Houghton Mifflin).

1961   O'Dell. *Island of the Blue Dolphins.* (Houghton Mifflin).

1960   Krumgold. *Onion John.* (Crowell).

1959   Speare. *The Witch of Blackbird Pond.* (Houghton Mifflin).

1958   Keith. *Rifles for Watie.* (Crowell).

1957   Sorenson. *Miracles on Maple Hill.* (Harcourt).

1956   Latham. *Carry On, Mr. Bowditch.* (Houghton Mifflin).

1955   DeJong. *The Wheel on the School.* (Harper).

1954   Krumgold. *... And Now Miguel.* (Crowell).

1953   Clark. *Secret of the Andes.* (Viking).

1952   Estes. *Ginger Pye.* (Harcourt).

1951   Yates. *Amos Fortune, Free Man.* (Dutton).

1950   de Angeli *The Door in the Wall.* (Doubleday).

1949   Henry. *King of the Wind.* (Rand McNally).

1948   Du Bois. *The Twenty-one Balloons.* (Viking).

1947   Bailey. *Miss Hickory.* (Viking).

1946   Lenski. *Strawberry Girl.* (Lippincott).

1945   Lawson. *Rabbit Hill.* (Viking).

1944   Forbes. *Johnny Tremain.* (Houghton Mifflin).

1943   Gray. *Adam of the Road.* (Viking).

1942   Edmonds. *The Matchlock Gun.* (Dodd, Mead).

1941   Sperry. *Call It Courage.* (Macmillan).

1940   Daugherty. *Daniel Boone.* (Viking).

1939   Enright. *Thimble Summer.* (Farrar & Rinehart).

1938   Seredy. *The White Stag.* (Viking).

1937   Sawyer. *Roller Skates.* (Viking).

1936   Brink. *Caddie Woodlawn.* (Macmillan).

1935   Shannon. *Dobry.* (Viking).

1934   Meigs. *Invincible Louisa.* (Little, Brown).

1933   Lewis. *Young Fu of the Upper Yangtze.* (Holt).

1932   Armer. *Waterless Mountain.* (McKay).

1931   Coatsworth. *The Cat Who Went to Heaven.* (Macmillan).

1930   Field. *Hitty.* (Macmillan).

1929   Kelly. *The Trumpeter of Krakow.* (Macmillan).

1928   Mukerji. *Gayneck: The Story of a Pigeon.* (Dutton).

1927   James. *Smoky, the Cowhorse.* (Scribner).

1926   Chrisman. *Shen of the Sea.* (Dutton).

1925   Finger. *Tales from Silver Lands.* (Doubleday).

1924   Hawes. *The Dark Frigate.* (Atlantic-Little, Brown).

1923   Lofting. *Voyages of Doctor Doolittle.* (Lippincott).

1922   Van Loon. *Story of Mankind.* (Liveright).

CALDECOTT MEDAL

1984   Provensen. *The Glorious Flight: Across the Channel with Louis Blériot.* (Viking).

1983   Brown. *Shadow.* (Scribner).

The Caldecott is awarded annually for the book with the "most distinguished" illustrations of the preceding year. Dates indicate year of award, not year of publication. Names are those of the books' illustrators.

1982	Van Allsburg. *Jumanji*. (Houghton Mifflin).
1981	Lobel. *Fables*. (Harper).
1980	Cooney. *Ox-Cart Man*. (Viking).
1979	Goble. *The Girl Who Loved Wild Horses*. (Bradbury).
1978	Spier. *Noah's Ark*. (Doubleday).
1977	Dillon and Dillon. *Ashanti to Zulu: African Traditions*. (Dial).
1976	Dillon and Dillon. *Why Mosquitos Buzz in People's Ears*. (Dial).
1975	McDermott. *Arrow to the Sun*. (Viking).
1974	Zemach. *Duffy and the Devil*. (Farrar).
1973	Lent. *Funny Little Woman*. (Dutton).
1972	Hogrogian. *One Fine Day*. (Macmillan).
1971	Haley. *A Story, a Story*. (Atheneum).
1970	Steig. *Sylvester and the Magic Pebble*. (Windmill/Simon & Schuster).
1969	Shulevitz. *Fool of the World and the Flying Ship*. (Farrar).
1968	Emberley. *Drummer Hoff*. (Prentice-Hall).
1967	Ness. *Sam, Bangs and Moonshine*. (Holt).
1966	Hogrogian. *Always Room for One More*. (Holt).
1965	Montressor. *May I Bring a Friend?* (Atheneum).
1964	Sendak. *Where the Wild Things Are*. (Harper).
1963	Keats. *The Snowy Day*. (Viking).
1962	Brown. *Once a Mouse*. (Scribner).
1961	Sidjakov. *Baboushka and the Three Kings*. (Parnassus/Houghton).
1960	Ets. *Nine Days to Christmas*. (Viking).
1959	Cooney. *Chanticleer and the Fox*. (Crowell).
1958	McCloskey. *Time of Wonder*. (Viking).
1957	Simont. *A Tree Is Nice*. (Harper).
1956	Rojankovsky. *Frog Went a-Courtin'*. (Harcourt).

1955   Brown. *Cinderella.* (Scribner).

1954   Bemelmans. *Madeline's Rescue.* (Viking).

1953   Ward. *The Biggest Bear.* (Houghton Mifflin).

1952   Nicolas. *Finders Keepers.* (Harcourt).

1951   Milhous. *The Egg Tree.* (Scribner).

1950   Politi. *Song of the Swallows.* (Scribner).

1949   Harder and Harder. *The Big Snow.* (Macmillan).

1948   Duvoisin. *White Snow, Bright Snow.* (Lothrop).

1947   Weisgard. *The Little Island.* (Doubleday).

1946   Petersham and Petersham. *The Rooster Crows.* (Macmillan).

1945   Jones. *Prayer for a Child.* (Macmillan).

1944   Slobodkin. *Many Moons.* (Harcourt).

1943   Burton. *The Little House.* (Houghton Mifflin).

1942   McCloskey. *Make Way for Ducklings.* (Viking).

1941   Lawson. *They Were Strong and Good.* (Viking).

1940   d'Aulaire and d'Aulaire. *Abraham Lincoln.* (Doubleday).

1939   Handforth. *Mei Lei.* (Doubleday).

1938   Lathrop. *Animals of the Bible.* (Lippincott).

HOLIDAY DATES, OBSERVANCES, AND EVENTS

April Fools' Day	April 1
Arbor Day	Last Friday in April; scheduled on other dates in some states
Armistice Day	November 11
Black History Month	February
Children's Book Week	2nd week in November
Christmas	December 25
Columbus Day	2nd Monday in October
Easter	1st Sunday after paschal full moon, in March or April (see almanac or calendar)
Election Day	1st Tuesday after 1st Monday in November
Fall	On or about September 22, the date of the autumnal equinox
Father's Day	3rd Sunday in June
Flag Day	June 14
Grandparents' Day	1st Sunday after Labor Day
Groundhog Day	February 2
Halloween	October 31
Hanukah	Eight days in November or December (see almanac or calendar)
Independence Day	July 4
Martin Luther King's Birthday	3rd Monday in January
Labor Day	1st Monday in September
Lincoln's Birthday	February 12 or 1st Monday in February

May Day	May 1
Memorial Day	Last Monday in May
Mother's Day	2nd Sunday in May
National Library Week	1st week in April
New Year's Day	January 1
St. Patrick's Day	March 17
Spring	On or about March 20, the date of the vernal equinox
Summer	On or about June 21, the date of the summer solstice
Thanksgiving	4th Thursday in November
United Nations Day	October 24
Valentine's Day	February 14
Veteran's Day	November 11 or 4th Monday of October
Washington's Birthday	3rd Monday in February
Winter	On or about December 21, the date of the winter solstice

—ANNOTATED BIBLIOGRAPHY—

This selected list of books, pertinent to many of the bulletin board ideas described in this book, are valuable for both instruction and inspiration.

Allport, Alan. *Paper Sculpture.* New York: Drake, 1971.
    Attractive and amusing pieces, i.e., kangaroo, page 33, and girl's head, page 36. Maybe too intricate for bulletin board use, but an asset to a library collection.

Ames, Lee J. *Draw 50 Famous Faces.* New York: Doubleday, 1978.
    One of a series of drawing instruction books. Includes Churchill, Dracula, W. C. Fields, Martin Luther King, Lincoln, George Washington, and many more.

Amidon, Eva V. *Easy Quillery.* New York: Morrow, 1977.
    Easy instructions for making paper coils and scrolls. Designed for children, with good instructions. Includes bee, page 94; Easter eggs, page 93; and lettering, page 60.

Better Homes & Gardens. *Holiday Decorations You Can Make.* New York: Meredith, 1974.
    Decorations that children can make. Includes pixies, page 91; Christmas stockings, pages 62-73; and paper ornaments, pages 168-71.

Biegeleisen, J. I. *The ABC of Lettering,* 5th edition. New York: Harper, 1976.
    A lettering sourcebook, practical and complete. A portfolio of alphabet styles.

Bottomley, Jim. *Paper Projects for Creative Kids of All Ages.* Boston: Little, Brown, 1983.
    An inventive book, heavily illustrated with drawings and photos. Includes large 3-D box letters, page 78; witch's cauldron and broom, pages 66 and 67; and a quilled racing turtle, page 48.

Boyd, Margaret A. *Catalog Sources for Creative People.* Tucson, Ariz.: H. P. Books, 1981.
    Over 2,000 listings of sources for patterns, plans, kits, and materials for arts and crafts.

Brock, Virginia. *Piñatas.* Nashville, Tenn.: Abingdon, 1966.
    All about piñatas. Directions for birthday cake, Easter egg, football, and witch piñatas, among many others.

Card and Cardboard Colorcraft. New York: Franklin Watts, 1971.
    Includes owl, page 122; knight's helmet, page 118.

Carroll, David. *Make Your Own Chess Set.* Englewood Cliffs, N.J.: Prentice-Hall, 1974.
    25 unique chess sets out of inexpensive materials.

Chaikin, Miriam. *Light Another Candle.* New York: Ticknor and Fields, 1981.
The story and meaning of Hanukah. Illustrated. Coins, page 65.

Churchill, Katherine. *Easy to Make Paper Art Activities for Holidays and Seasons.* Paoli, Penna.: Instructo/McGraw-Hill, 1978.
Ideas for many things, not wordy, easy. Contains pinwheel, page 64; chain caterpillar, page 74; butterflies of papier-mâché, page 73; chicks, page 71; scarecrow, page 23; and skeletons, page 28.

Comins, Jeremy. *Slotted Sculpture from Cardboard.* New York: Lothrop, Lee & Shepard, 1977.
Directions for constructing animals, people, and everyday objects by slotting together ordinary cardboard.

Constas, Dorothy. *Treasury of Arts and Crafts Paper Projects for the Elementary School.* West Nyack, N.Y.: Parker, 1977.
122 lessons, classroom tested. Projects can be correlated with subjects. Includes lessons, materials, and procedures. Useful to librarians and teachers.

Cornell, Jane. *Art of Gift Wrapping.* New York: Warner, 1980.
Inspirational for bulletin board ideas.

D'Amato, Janet and Alex. *Colonial Crafts for You to Make.* New York: Messner, 1975.
Easy instructions for making a variety of colonial items to use in displays. The theme is home and hearth.

_____ *More Colonial Crafts for You to Make.* New York: Messner, 1977.
More very easy instructions for items related to education (Hornbook), crafts, amusements, and toys.

Drehman, Vera L. *Holiday Ornaments from Paper Scraps.* New York: Hearthside, 1970.
Bat pattern, page 136; bats in a cave, page 116.

Eckstein, Artis Aleene, Heidi Borchers, and Tiffany Windsor. *Super Scrap-Craft Book.* New York: New American Library, 1983.
Includes lamb, made with paper plates, page 27; mouse, page 30. Paper plate flowers, page 26, are useful for bulletin boards.

Eisner, Vivienne, and Adelle Weiss. *The Newspaper Everything Book.* New York: Dutton, 1975.
How to make 150 useful objects from old newspapers, including neckties and three-cornered hat.

Fabri, Ralph. *Sculpture in Paper.* New York: Watson-Guptill, 1966.
Contains many items useful to the librarian in making displays. A gorgeous turkey is pictured on page 67.

Ficarotta, Phyllis. *Treasury of Craft Designs.* New York: Bantam, 1973.
 Craft creations from inexpensive or throwaway materials.

Fisher, Leonard Everett. *Alphabet Art.* New York: Four Winds, 1978.
 13 ABC's from around the world. Includes information on each alphabet and its origins. The actual foreign-language letters are large and easy to trace, and can be further enlarged using an opaque projector.

Fowler, Virginie. *Paperworks.* Englewood Cliffs, N.J.: Prentice-Hall, 1982.
 Includes items from picture eggs to fish kites. Paper doll pattern and instruction for enlargement is on page 72.

Gallivan, Marion F. *Fun for Kids.* Metuchen, N.J.: Scarecrow, 1981.
 An index to children's craft books—300 in all, indexed according to item and craft material.

Grainger, Stuart E. *Creative Papercraft.* New York: Sterling, 1980.
 A beautiful book. Heraldic devices in relief. Stag and Tudor Rose and Panther Rampant, on pages 28 and 29, are stunning. Also includes aquarium figures in relief, and St. George and the dragon patterns.

Grater, Michael. *Paper Faces.* New York: Taplinger, 1968.
 Paper faces: animals and holiday figures, all cut from plain paper. Masks, too.

———— *Paper Play.* New York: Taplinger, 1972.
 Imaginative book about paper, the most important ingredient in the making of bulletin boards. Contains many ideas, tips, and techniques for the manipulation of paper.

Hartung, Ralph. *Creating with Corrugated Paper.* New York: Reinhold, 1966.
 Inspiration for making many things, including Muiredach Cross.

Harvey, Michael. *Lettering Design.* New York: Bonanza, 1980.
 Basic forms, variations, and design criteria of lettering. Contains model alphabets.

Hawkinson, John. *Pastels Are Great!* Chicago: Albert Whitman, 1968.
 How-to book, teaching children the art of drawing with pastels.

Ives, Suzy. *Making Paper Flowers and Decorations.* New York: Taplinger, 1973.
 Patterns and instructions for making a variety of paper flowers in a simple and inexpensive manner.

Janitch, Valerie. *All Made from Paper.* New York: Viking, 1974.
 A beautifully illustrated book. Paper pictures (collage), mobiles, fairytale castle, stained glass method, celtic cross, flowers, etc.

Janvier, Jeannine. *Fabulous Birds You Can Make.* New York: Sterling, 1976.
  Adapt construction for floating swans, page 18, to make ducklings in Mother's Day board, page 154.

Kirsch, Dietrich, and Jutta Kirsch-Korn. *Make Your Own Paper Flowers.* New York: Watson-Guptill, 1969.
  17 flower ideas, including interesting loop flowers on page 54.

Kramer, Jack. *Silhouettes.* Boston: Houghton-Mifflin, 1977.
  How to make silhouettes and paper sculptures. Contains a gallery of selective patterns. Interesting items are the alligator, page 118; the lion, page 122; and the butterfly, page 127.

Laliberté, Norman, and Alex Mogdon. *Silhouettes.* New York: Reinhold, 1968.
  Includes faces, page 44; profiles, page 48; flag, page 104; and valentine, page 92.

Munson, D. *The Paper Book.* New York: Scribner, 1970.
  187 things to make with paper. Good instructions.

Newman, Thelma R., Gay Hartley Newman, and Lee Scott Newman. *Paper as Art and Craft.* New York: Crown, 1973.
  Complete book of the history and processes of the paper arts. The quilted newspaper collage on page 161, in which padding is done with tissue paper, is particularly interesting.

Parish, Peggy. *Costumes to Make.* New York: Macmillan, 1970.
  Costume books often provide a good source for bulletin board items. See the witch's hat, page 41; the Santa hat, page 52; and the tricorn hat, vest, and ruff, page 20.

Pauli, Anna E., and Margaret S. Mitzit. *How to Make Paper Figures.* Minneapolis, Minn.: Dennison, 1979.
  An excellent book of instructions for making animals and figures. The pictured products are appealing and professional looking. Particularly interesting and useful are the box-based Children of the World, page 71, and Spike, the Turkey, page 97.

Pen and Brush Lettering and Alphabets, 15th edition. Poole, Dorset, Great Britain, Blandford, 1970.
  Contains 50 alphabets, easy to trace or enlarge with the opaque projector.

Perry, Margaret. *Rainy Day Magic.* New York: Lippincott, 1970.
  Good crackerbox creations, from the ark to a village schoolhouse.

Portchmouth, John. *All Kinds of Papercrafts.* New York: Viking, 1972.
  A practical and inspirational book full of ideas on how to do many things with paper.

Purdy, Susan. *Costumes for You to Make.* New York: Lippincott, 1971.
  Contains instructions for many hats and shoes, and also military medals, on page 53.

———— *Holiday Cards for You to Make.* New York: Lippincott, 1967.
    A good idea book for bulletin board displays.

Rockland, Mae Shafter. *The Hanukkah Book.* New York: Schocken, 1975.
    Complete Hanukkah book: origins, lights, festivities. Contains many craft ideas.

Romberg, Jenean. *Let's Discover Paper.* New York: Center for Applied Research in Education, 1975.
    Inventive methods a child can use. See beautiful and easy fruit, page 59; standing animals, page 41; and flowers, page 35.

Rosse, Allianora, and Don Munson. *The Paper Book.* New York: Scribner, 1970.
    187 things to make, including peacock plumes on page 113.

Roth, Dandra, and Beverly Bicker. *Creative Gift Wrapping.* Charlotte, N.C.: East Woods, 1982.
    A highly imaginative book with patterns and ideas for all occasions.

Sattler, Helen Roney. *Holiday Gifts, Favors and Decorations.* New York: Lothrop, Lee & Shephard, 1971.
    Enlarges on many ideas for holidays throughout the year.

Stephan, Barbara B. *Creating with Tissue Paper.* New York: Crown, 1973.
    Full of good ideas for designs and technique. Contains a large variety of flowers.

Torbet, Laura. *How to Do Everything with Markers.* New York: Bobbs-Merrill, 1976.
    An excellent resource for patterns, ideas, alphabets. Peacock lampshade instructions, pages 55-57, can be adapted for Peacocks and Lilies bulletin board on page 141.

Wankelman, Williard F., and Philip Wigg. *A Handbook of Arts and Crafts for Elementary and High School Teachers,* 5th ed. Dubuque, Iowa: William C. Brown, 1982.
    Particularly useful is the section on cut-paper lettering. Other notables are matting and framing pictures, and paper script.

Wood, Louise and Orvello. *Make It with Paper.* New York: David McKay, 1970.
    Basic patterns and techniques for making a wide variety of paper objects. A particularly practical and useful book.

Weiss, Harvey. *Working with Cardboard and Paper.* Reading, Mass.: Addison-Wesley, 1978.
    Includes houses, castles, airplanes, cars, boats, and trains.

Working with Paper. New York: Watts, 1971.
    Paper projects from simple to advanced. Step-by-step color illustrations and photos.

–INDEX–